The Joys and Terrors of Public  Speaking

By David Scott

ISBN: 978-1-291-80373-0

PublishNation, London

www.publishnation.co.uk

This book is dedicated to the memory of Roger Collins, Pat Mead and David Lomas – good friends who died far too early.

INTRODUCTION

If you don't read the newspaper you are uninformed, if you do read the newspaper you are misinformed. -- Mark Twain

I was busy preparing to give a talk to Torquay Probus Club one Thursday morning when I realised what interesting people I had met and the fun I had had when giving talks to such groups. It made me wonder if other local newspaper editors, past and present, along with the friends I knew who carried out public speaking engagements, had also had similar experiences.

My interest aroused, I dashed off a few emails to those I thought would soon let me know whether the idea was worth pursuing and almost immediately the answer they gave was a resounding *'yes'*.

'If newspaper editors don't have any anecdotes, who does? ' was a typical reply.

Encouraged by the response, I set out to unearth a treasure trove of stories which I felt deserved a wider audience. As far as I know this collection is the first time such stories have been gathered together in one place. I hope they not only give an insight into how difficult public speaking can be, but how fraught an experience it can be for those involved – both speakers and audiences.

I encouraged contributors to tell their stories in their own words and most did. A few were happy to be interviewed. Apart from the occasional comma or full stop, I have kept to the original copy they sent me.

I would like to think that new generations of editors and other public speakers will find this book a useful guide to what they might expect when leaving the comfort of their warm offices for draughty village halls and sometimes unforgiving audiences.

I have included my list of list of do's and do nots of public speaking to which others have added their own favourites. It is by no means an exhaustive list.

My own experiences as a newspaper editor taught me that a journalist's sense of what is or is not funny is generally totally different from the public's. A joke that has the news room splitting its sides quite often falls flat when told to an outsider - as my wife will testify. Despite this I have included a glossary of jokes sent to me over the years which can be used by speakers, depending on the audience they are addressing. However, the art of being able to tell a joke rather that just reading it is something that often only comes with experience and even then is best avoided by those who cannot pause in the right places and place emphasis on the right words.

I owe a big 'thank you' to all those who have been willing to give up their time to write about their experiences and for the enjoyment they have given me when reading their efforts. If nothing else, it has been good to learn that I am not alone in finding public speaking an interesting way to gain an insight into the great British public.

Mind you, not every editor enjoys giving talks about their newspaper and their work. **Anita Syvret, former editor of the Gloucestershire Echo,** told me: '*I was never a fan of the after-dinner speaking rigmarole. I only ever agreed to do questions and answer sessions – and if the audience didn't have any questions, I went back to the office and left them to their bacon and eggs. And jokes? I never told any. Sorry.* '

She is not alone. Some of the people I asked to contribute said they didn't have any experience worth passing on, while others told me they regarded public speaking as a chore or something that went with the job. A few admitted they took the opportunity to delegate all speaker requests to either their deputy or some other member of staff. I have been fortunate to get contributions from these 'volunteers'.

I have not made any mention in this book about speakers' fees. A celebrity can charge a four figure fee plus travel and accommodation costs. This book has deliberately avoided such people, interesting though some, but not all, of them might be. A few well known speakers enjoy a free cruise in lieu of any fee, although judging by the cruises I have been on there has been a reduction in the number of speakers invited to enjoy such hospitality and a definite drop in the quality of what they have to say!

I never charged a fee when I was invited to speak in my capacity as editor of various local newspapers; I felt it was a duty that really did come with the job. On most such occasions I enjoyed it. Nowadays I do charge, except when invited to speak to an organisation which has me as one of its members. Any fee I get only covers basic costs such as petrol and a lunch-time meal for my wife and I. One year recently I made enough for us to have a weekend break in a top class hotel.

I have been encouraged by the number of times some organisations have invited me back. I have three staple talks open to anyone brave enough to invite me: Life on a Local Newspaper; Was the First World War Inevitable?; The Falklands after the 1982 War.

I hope you get as much enjoyment out of reading what has happened to some speakers as I have done in collating their written efforts.

CHAPTER ONE

PERSONALLY SPEAKING

Members of the audience are always right. Sometimes confused, mis-informed, rude, stubborn, changeable and even downright stupid. But never wrong. – The sign on my desk to remind me of some basic truths.

I was 18 years old when I first addressed an audience of any kind. I was extremely nervous beforehand, but once I got into my stride most, but not all, of my nerves disappeared. I am just the same today despite many years of facing hostile, sometimes sceptical, but generally friendly groups assembled to hear what I have to say. The nerves are still there to a greater or lesser degree; I console myself that is a good state to be in because it means I will give my best and not take any audience for granted.

The common fear of public speaking is called glossophobia. Some people know it as "stage fright," although many people simply confuse normal nerves and anxiety with a genuine phobia.

That first step into the unknown was at a public meeting in 1966 called by Barnoldswick Young Liberals to campaign for more social amenities and a public swimming baths in the town. We were an idealistic and very naive group of young people who scared the pants off the establishment running our small town on the border of Yorkshire and Lancashire. Barnoldswick was a 'neglected' town with a small urban council that provided the minimum of local services and contented itself with emptying the dustbins and providing work for a small group of bureaucrats. It had no chance of raising the money that would be needed to improve recreational facilities until it was absorbed into Pendle District Council in 1974, so our efforts didn't get anywhere at the time but paved the way for a future campaign which achieved its objective when a new pool was attached to the town's secondary modern school in the 1980s. I spoke for 10 minutes and tried to rouse the audience into an indignant frenzy. There was more passion than hard facts.

More importantly, as far as I was concerned, I got a taste for public speaking and telling a story. It stood me in good stead when I fought the Braintree seat at the February 1974 General Election, became the editor of a weekly newspaper in Romford a few months later and a councillor in Maldon, Essex, soon after that.

The Barnoldswick establishment got some sort of revenge on me a few months after that initial speech when I addressed the town's rotary club lunch and outlined the work I – a very junior reporter – did for the wonderfully named Barnoldswick and Earby Times. As I was leaving the town clerk took me on one side and said: '*We prefer our speakers to wear a tie that is properly knotted and a shirt where the top button is fastened.*' From that day on I have never given a talk while not wearing a tie and I would advise any male speaker who is in doubt to wear one! I learned to tie a very good Windsor knot.

In those days I listened to far more speeches than I gave. As a young reporter I attended school speech days, council meetings, public meetings and court hearings. School speech days were by far the worst. I had no choice but to listen to six of them while a pupil at Ermysted's Skipton Grammar School and not one left any impression. The school seemed to delight in inviting back ex pupils all of whom had marvellous academic achievements but few oratory skills. Attendance was compulsory and woe betide anyone who dared not turn up.

Many years later I was on the school's shortlist to be the guest speaker at the 1985 speech day when by then I was Managing Director of a newspaper group in the Midlands. But the invitation never came. I was quietly told that only those who had gone on to one of the better universities got an invitation to speak at such a prestigious event! There was no way at that time that somebody who left with seven O'Levels and chose to serve a three-and-half-year apprenticeship on a local newspaper instead of doing A Levels was going to be invited back.

I had to do my fair share of court reporting during my first 12 months as a cub reporter, but was not disappointed when I was switched to sports reporting and only went to court when the office was short of staff. Most of the cases were relatively minor – drunkeness, theft, driving offences etc – only enlivened one memorable day when the local streaker was eventually brought to trial. The defendant had run naked through a village for some months before he was spotted by a policeman. For reasons nobody could understand the streaker climbed up a tree and defied anybody to get him down. The brave policeman took off his jacket and climbed after him. In the ensuing struggle the streaker grabbed the policeman in a painful place, but was eventually brought down to earth. When the senior magistrate gave him a heavy fine he also delivered a lengthy speech about how such behaviour would not be tolerated and during it warned: ' *You must learn young man that you cannot take the law into your own hands.*' The public gallery erupted in laughter, while the court officials and solicitors tried hard not to follow. The magistrate remained stony-faced. Perhaps it is a good job I did not shout out: '*What bare-faced cheek*' or I might have been brought in front of the magistrate for contempt of court.

Listening to speeches, given by the average solicitor (especially for the defence) on an ordinary court day tried my patience. I could not agree more with the California Attorney General who said: '*An incompetent lawyer can delay a case for months, but a competent one can delay it even longer!*' Thank goodness I was not the reporter when one eminent barrister took 17 days to deliver his final speech – and still lost the case!

'*Words are a lawyer's tools of trade*,' said the late Lord Denning and nothing illustrates that more than a short speech made in an Irish court in 1860 which is still trotted out today. A lawyer named Webb was applying for a licence for a public house in the city on behalf of a 25-year-old man. The police objected to the licence on the grounds of the man's age and the judge was similarly inclined until Mr Webb stood up and said: '*Alexander the Great when aged 22 crushed the Illyrians, razed the city of Thebes to the ground, conquered Darius and brought the great Persian empire under his control. At 23 Rene Descartes evolved a new system of philosophy. At 24 Pitt was the prime Minister of Great Britain. At 24 Napoleon overthrew his enemies with a whiff of grapeshot in Paris. Is it now to be judicially decided that this man at the age of 25 is too young to manage a public house?*' The speech lasted 45 seconds and won the argument and the man his licence.

My favourite court speech, however, came at a Scottish trial. The accused awaited his sentence from the sheriff and feared the worst. As he stood in the dock he was surprised when the sheriff told him: '*Although I find you a fecund liar, I will not send you to prison.* ' The man expressed his thanks with the words: '*Thank you, your honour, and you are a fecund good judge!*'

Once my journalistic apprenticeship was up and I was now a fully fledged senior reporter I moved 300 miles south in December 1969 to become sports editor and then deputy editor of the Maldon and Burnham Standard in Essex, where I soon had to develop my public speaking skills very quickly because I received a variety of invitations to attend and speak at dinners, end-of-season presentations and finals nights across a wide range of sports.

Naively I thought word had got around that I was an entertaining speaker until someone who had too much to drink at one football club dinner told me that by inviting me they felt they were guaranteed a picture and report in the following Thursday's paper.

I was able to continue my political activities in an area where only a very small band of supporters kept the Liberal banner flying. I fought and lost a couple of by-elections in an attempt to become the only Liberal member of the old Maldon Urban Council (abolished in 1973) and then out of the blue was selected as Parliamentary candidate for the newly created seat of Braintree, which had an even smaller band of Liberal supporters. Fortunately they more than made up for their lack of numbers with their hard working efforts on both my and the party's behalf.

By the 1970s there were few public meetings involving ordinary Parliamentary candidates during a General Election campaign. Television had taken over and political debating was mainly conducted on screen and the more serious radio programmes. If you booked a village hall you were lucky if more than half a dozen members of the public turned up along with your own supporters and a couple of people sent by the opposition to heckle you.

The one exception at that time came during a 1973 by-election in the Isle of Ely when television broadcaster, newspaper columnist and celebrity chef Clement Freud was the Liberal candidate. Freud placed a bet at 33-1 to win the seat, which he duly did. His celebrity status attracted good audiences and he repaid their support with some entertaining comments. However, he was not a farmer and knew little about sugar beet so the Tories ensured he faced some awkward questions at every meeting. The crunch came the night before polling at a meeting in Ely Town hall when more than 1,000 people turned up to hear Freud and Liberal leader David Steel. Sure enough a well known local farmer stood up and asked a tough question on sugar beet. Freud gave him one of his famous hound-dog looks and said: *"Ladies and gentleman, if you still need to be convinced I am the man to vote for tomorrow, look at this man. He is one of the area's leading experts on sugar beet and he is asking me for advice."* The farmer sat down - the audience loved it

I did all my campaigning and speaking on the doorstep. It worked in my favour because both my opponents – Tony Newton (Conservative) and Keith Kyle (Labour) - were accomplished public speakers and were hot on their respective parties' policies. Tony Newton, who became the MP, was straight out of the Tory party's research department, while Keith Kyle was a well known television reporter and very able in front of an audience of any size and a television camera. All I had was enthusiasm.

We shared only one platform on the 'soft' subject of international aid and help for other countries organised by some obscure pressure group. It was not a subject I was over familiar with but I did some homework and spoke adequately enough to satisfy my supporters who hogged the front row. They thought they were giving me moral support; I would have preferred them to have been elsewhere. That election in Braintree, at least, was remarkable because all three candidates got on well whenever we met and were polite to each other.

The count took place on the day after the election because the Braintree constituency at that time covered a huge geographical area containing many villages. I had to stand in front of a large crowd outside Braintree Town Hall early on the Friday afternoon and give what is known as the loser's speech. I was tired, disappointed I had not won (although I came within 5,000 votes of causing a major upset) and just wanted to go home and sleep. However, one's duty meant I had to cheer up my hardy band of enthusiastic supporters so I told them that Mr Newton was keeping the seat warm for me and next time we would get him. I could not have been more wrong - he remained Braintree's MP for 23 years until being ousted by a Labour candidate in the Tory's 1997 General Election debacle.

There was a second General Election in 1974 but I was not the Braintree Liberal candidate, having opted for a journalistic rather than a political career and been appointed editor of the Romford Observer. The Liberal Party invited me to speak at my successor Richard (now Lord) Holmes' adoption meeting and then give a short rallying call at another adoption meeting of a candidate who, to save his blushes, I will not name. The said candidate had three stock answers to any questions put to him at such meetings:

1. I agree with you.
2. Isn't that awful?
3. I will look into that.

Unfortunately for him the meeting was better attended than most because of a hot local issue involving local schools and his three answers began to wear a bit thin. When one woman asked what he thought about stricter discipline in primary and junior schools he saw his chance to offer something different and replied that he was in favour of ' *the re-introduction of capital punishment in schools'*. The woman kept a straight face and said: ' *I take it from that you favour hanging five-and-six-year olds.*' He lost his deposit in the ensuing election.

My hopes of making an impact on the national stage were over but the Romford Observer's owners did not mind me becoming involved in local politics, particularly as Romford is in the London borough of Havering and Maldon, where I lived, is 45 miles away on the Essex coast - the two might as well be on different planets

I duly got elected to Maldon District Council at a by-election for the Heybridge ward in 1975 after making yet another loser's speech the year before when I came up just one vote short after three recounts, one of which had me ahead. Trying to remain cheerful at 2am was not easy!

It was while on the council I discovered that if I had a serious message I wanted to get across I needed to pepper my comments and speeches with some humour. It proved to be a great way to either disarm or infuriate my critics and helped me play a leading part within a small opposition group that challenged the ruling Tories on the council. I was the only Liberal councillor for three years but I joined forces with a handful of Independents, two Labour councillors and one renegade Conservative to have some fun with stuffy councillors who failed to enter into the spirit of things and definitely had no sense of humour. We often won the argument but not the vote!

Perhaps the moment I enjoyed best, and caused plenty of giggles among the officers and the public gallery came when the council congratulated two councillors who had claimed a cash reward for apprehending a teenager who was kicking hell out of the ladies toilet doors in a public car park late one night. The councillors were sat in a car discussing what had gone on at a planning meeting when they noticed what the young man was intent on doing, so out they leapt and frogmarched him to the nearby police station. The reward was intended for members of the public, but the councillors claimed it from their own council and donated it to charity when the teenager was convicted. I had to put up with several minutes of public spirit/union flag waving before I stood up and said that *'as leader of the Liberal group on the council (I was the only one) I wished to add my congratulations to the two councillors and hoped that in the best interests of the town they would continue to hang around the ladies' toilets in the car park.'* The committee chairman and some of his colleagues had yet another fit and sense of humour loss; one councillor was so outraged he told me I was not a gentleman!

During this time one group I addressed at least once a year to update them on council and other matters was the Heybridge Darby and Joan Club. This involved a 30 minute talk followed by questions. They were a lovely group of older citizens who helped give me a

11

massive majority when I stood for re-election in 1979. After one such talk an elderly lady came up to tell me how much she had enjoyed the Liberal Christmas bazaar a few months earlier when I had sold her some excellent *'right handed tea cups.'* She wanted to know if I had any left handed ones?

I also had some fun during my Mayoral year 1979/80. I was the youngest ever Mayor of Maldon and only got the position because of a split in the Tory ranks. While I took my duties seriously, I also enjoyed some light-hearted moments. The best came when the town's Plume Library re-opened after renovation. The Lord Lieutenant was invited and because he was there the organisers felt they should hire a toastmaster to introduce everyone and run the proceedings. Unfortunately when it came to him asking for silence he brought his gavel down on the new counter made of glass and it shattered into lots of pieces. I managed to keep a straight face - just. Whatever I said was surely lost on my audience after that performance.

Public speaking had to be taken seriously during the Mayoral year and some tough lessons had to be learned. Inevitably, I got caught out more than once. Nobody told me tradition dictated that as guest speaker at the Royal Naval Association dinner I had to stay until the end because when I left the event was over. It had been a particularly tiring Saturday with Mayoral events morning, afternoon and evening and by 11pm my wife and I were ready for home. I duly did my speaking bit, chatted a while longer and even had a couple of dances but then told the chairman we would be leaving quietly. I could tell by the look on his face that something was wrong. When I discovered what was likely to happen if we left I sat down again, the band played on and we didn't leave until 1.30am.

During that hectic year, which involved making at least one major and several minor speeches a week, we were invited to Malden in Massachusetts on an official visit. A couple of weeks before my wife and I were due to fly out the telephone rang at 2am. At first I ignored it, thinking it was a wrong number, but when it rang again I went down to the lounge while still naked to find one of Boston's major radio stations on line asking me to give a 10 minute talk on the town of Maldon and then take part in a 20 minute discussion with Malden Mayor Jim Conway. I went 'live' inside a minute. Fortunately I quickly managed to engage my brain and assemble some information to educate our American cousins. Mayor Conway and I then proceeded to have our chat about the two towns and politics while I got colder and colder. It was quite surreal. Finally, the call came to an end with the radio station wishing me *'bon voyage'* and playing Rule Britannia down the line from 3,000 miles away. You couldn't have made it up. When we made the official visit the radio station discovered I had been naked all the time I had chatted and sent me two of their large t-shirts *'to cover my embarrassment'* should they ring again!

While in the United States I spoke at twelve public engagements varying from business to sport to youth groups and the local council. On several occasions I had just one day's notice about whom I would be speaking to which meant I had to put together the required words in much haste. I learned the hard way that British humour often attracts blank looks from Americans. They don't understand irony and I soon gave up trying to 'entertain' them with any of the jokes I had packed in my suitcase. Even a quip that *'George the third made a big mistake so could we now have the country back '* didn't excite them.

My final talk on what was a memorable American trip came during a morning service on the last Sunday before we headed home when in front of a packed church I had to address the congregation from the pulpit. I had never before stood in a pulpit and found it quite different from any other speaking experience. I cannot explain why it was different – it just was.

In 1980 I became editor of the Banbury Guardian in Oxfordshire, a large broadsheet paper with a long tradition of being heavily involved in the community. It was while speaking to rotary, probus, WI and meetings of other organisations in the Banbury area I realised that while audiences like to be educated, they also want speakers to entertain them, so I started to build up a library of jokes and funny stories. I like to think that since then I have left a smile on most people's faces after one of my talks.

The Guardian's editor was also expected to chair any serious public meetings. My experience on Maldon Council was put to good use in controlling some quiet rowdy audiences when a funny quip often helped to defuse some heated rows.

In 1984 I helped launch and then edit Britain's first free daily newspaper – the Birmingham Daily News. It was an experiment that paved the way for the now highly successful free Metro range of daily newspapers in most English cities. However, the newspaper establishment at that time did not like the concept at all and the venture came under severe attack. I was nominated to be the public spokesman for the Daily News after all the senior management team spent a week in London undergoing extensive public speaking and television training. It was an experience which persuaded some of the team they would never go in front of a television camera again! I found the training invaluable, right down to what to wear and how to look at an audience. However, it did not stop me slipping up while taking part in a BBC documentary on the running of beauty competitions. The Miss Birmingham contest attracted 140 entrants via the Daily News and I was chairman of the panel that had to whittle that number down to 10. I was asked on camera how we decided which girls should go through to the final and without thinking said: *'I am delighted we have chosen girls you could find on any Birmingham street.'*

The traditional newspaper groups at that time were very suspicious of what we were up to and (rightly) worried about the impact it would have on their own daily newspapers. I was in great demand to speak at conferences and one occasion I came in for some tough questioning at an all-editors conference. Afterwards one of the few friendly faces came up to me and said: *'Remember, David, that the collective noun for a group of editors is an arrogance!'*

The bravest conference speech I have ever heard was delivered at a Northcliffe newspapers conference held in Bath just before the 1999 solar eclipse. One of the sessions involved editors giving a 15 minute presentation on a subject chosen for them by head office. It was a task few enjoyed and many badly stumbled over. One Cornish editor was told to speak on the subject *'What will the eclipse in Cornwall be like for you?'* The idea was for him to outline his newspaper's plans for coverage leading up to and beyond the event. At the appointed time the editor stepped forward holding two circular sheets of paper – one white, one black. He stood for a moment and then slowly let the black sheet move in front of and over the white sheet and then out the other side until his arms were fully crossed. His performance over, he sat down. There was stunned silence. Nobody dared laugh, although one or two shoulders were twitching. His bosses were not amused, but he had earned himself a few pints later in the evening from his fellow editors. It did not come as a surprise when he took early retirement soon after!

In 1987 I was asked to travel all the way to Australia to give three 35 minute talks about the Daily News. Two were at Melbourne University while the third was an address to the Pacific Area Newspaper Publishers Association conference in Adelaide, the organisers of which gave me a round the world first class air ticket for my troubles. The Adelaide talk in front of more than one thousand delegates was the only time I was genuinely frightened beforehand. I don't mean the usual pre-talk nerves but real fright.

Half an hour before I was due on stage I went to my hotel room and gave myself a good talking to along the lines of ... *'You haven't come all this way to make a hash of it now!'* After I had spoken the chairman asked me to stand with him so people could come and chat about any aspect of my talk. Most people were kind and thanked me for coming such a long way, but one man hovered at the sides and I could hear him muttering ... *'not very interesting,'* ' *don't know why he bothered travelling that far,' heard better'* etc etc. I tried to ignore him but eventually I asked the chairman who he was. *'Oh! Take no notice of him,* 'he said, *'He only repeats what everyone else is saying'*. It taught me a lesson about some of the votes of thanks I have received over the years.

One speaking engagement I enjoyed while editing the Daily News and then becoming its managing director was to address - on two occasions - senior boys in Rugby School's main hall on business and marketing techniques. Afterwards over a cup of tea the departmental head who had invited me said: ' *You know you spoke from exactly the same spot as Sir Winston Churchill when he came here'*.

Churchill is one of the people I most admire – along With Abraham Lincoln - for his ability to think quickly on his feet and give the sort of reply which demolished anyone trying to get one over him. I could never hope to match his oratorical skills. George Bernard Shaw once sent him two tickets for the opening night of his new play. He included a message which read: ' *Bring a friend if you have one'*. Churchill replied with a curt telegram which read: ' *Regret cannot attend your play tonight. Will come to second performance, if there is one.'*

Two of his best put-downs, which I often quote during my talks, are regarded as politically incorrect nowadays because both the recipients were women. Bessie Braddock, the outspoken Liverpool Labour MP from 1945 to 1970, accused Churchill of being drunk to which he responded: ' *Madam, you are ugly. But in the morning I shall be sober.'* This followed a clash a number of years earlier with another female MP, Nancy Astor who told him: ' *Sir, if you were my husband I would give you poison'* and he replied: ' *If I were your husband I would take it.'* Wonderful wit of which our current crop of politicians come nowhere near matching.

Churchill's speeches, especially during World War Two, were not only masterpieces in their own right but were badly needed to raise morale. His Premiership followed that of the unfortunate Neville Chamberlain who on his return from meeting Adolf Hitler in Munich in 1938 gave what must rank as one of the most naive speeches in history.

Chamberlain was initially acclaimed when he said: '*We, the German Führer and Chancellor, and the British Prime Minister, have had a further meeting today and are agreed in recognising that the question of Anglo-German relations is of the first importance for two countries and for Europe.*

"We regard the agreement signed last night and the Anglo-German Naval Agreement as symbolic of the desire of our two peoples never to go to war with one another again.

"We are resolved that the method of consultation shall be the method adopted to deal with any other questions that may concern our two countries, and we are determined to continue our efforts to remove possible sources of difference, and thus to contribute to assure the peace of Europe.

"My good friends this is the second time in our history that there has come back from Germany to Downing Street peace with honour. I believe it is peace in our time."

As we know, he could not have been more wrong. While I have made my own wild statements over the years, none has matched that.

I left the Daily News in 1988 to set up my own company and two years later my wife and I with three children in tow moved to live in Torquay. We arrived three days before Christmas. I wasn't to know it then but the town's main church, Upton Vale Baptist, was to be the venue for me to listen and learn from two of the best speakers I have ever had the privilege of hearing. If anyone wants to know what a good sermon sounds like then I have no hesitation in putting forward the names of the Rev. Andrew Green and the Rev. David Coffey. Andrew was (and still is) the senior pastor. David was his predecessor who had moved on to be general secretary of the Baptist Union of Great Britain and then President of the World Baptist Alliance by the time we landed in Torquay, but is still making regular appearances in the Upton Vale pulpit after moving back to South Devon upon his retirement. Their clear enunciation of the Bible and Christian teachings, and their ability to make what they are saying relevant to a modern audiences, have taught me a lot about the art of good public speaking. I am delighted both have contributed to this book.

Until then I had not been too impressed with most of the sermons I had had to sit through, starting with those delivered by my headmaster at Ermysted's Grammar School. The start-of-the day assemblies were dire. Five mornings a week we stood for 15 minutes while we sang two hymns and listened to the head explain some passage from the Bible at the end of which he would announce who he wanted to see in his study straight afterwards to be caned. He managed the transition from preaching to whacking quite smoothly, but it didn't impress me. There was hardly a morning when some unfortunate was not publicly named and shamed and some days as many as half a dozen pupils were lined up for 'execution'. I managed to avoid the cane, but it wasn't because I prayed a lot.

I found Devon audiences different from those in the Midlands. I soon learnt that I had to be prepared for all eventualities. One Tuesday afternoon I spoke to a Babbacombe ladies group. I was duly introduced by the chairman and was five minutes into my talk when I saw her gesticulating wildly from the back of the hall. When I stopped in mid sentence fearing a fire had broken out or even something worse, she dashed to the front and said: ' *Sorry I forgot. These ladies never listen to anyone unless they have had their cup of tea and a biscuit.*' At that point they all got up and went for their tea. I sat on the edge of the stage pretending to read my notes for 20 minutes at which point the chairman said: ' *Right you can continue now from where you left off.*'

I have been fortunate in that as far as I know I have only ever 'bombed' on one occasion and it was an experience I hope I will never repeat again. Soon after moving to Torquay I was invited to speak at Torquay Golf Club's annual dinner. The meal seemed to take an age to be served during which several of those present drank and drank and drank so that when the time came for me to stand up and address them all they wanted to do was bore the rest of their table with their very loud conversations. To make matters worse I was given a hand microphone which meant I could not turn the pages of my speech very easily. I eventually gave up even trying and ad libbed my way through what I knew was a dreadful performance. I have never used a hand microphone since.

I consoled myself that two of the greatest speakers the world has ever known also experienced times when they felt they had not delivered what their audiences expected. Abraham Lincoln's two minute Gettysburg Address on November 19 1863 is now regarded as one of the greatest speeches, but was severely criticised by newspapers of that time as being totally inadequate. Lincoln took to the stage after the previous speaker's two hour effort so you would have thought his audience and the journalists present would have welcomed such brevity.

The same could be said of Martin Luther King's ' *I have a dream'* speech on August 28 1963 in front of 250,000 people in Washington. He bored his audience for nine minutes as he rambled on - applause was light. If he had stopped then the speech would have been considered a monumental flop by a nationwide television audience. But as we know the next seven minutes galvanised the civil rights movement.

My bad night out was nothing compared to that of the Professional Footballers Association in 2013 when they invited black comedian Reginald D.Hunter to be the main speaker at their awards evening in London. Mr Hunter is best known for his appearances on television's Have I got News for You and Live at the Apollo. The PFA should have known what they would get. Apparently not!

PFA chairman Clarke Carlisle admitted it was a *'gross error of judgement'* to invite Mr Hunter after a media storm following some of the black comedian's 'jokes'. The PFA said it was 'totally dismayed' by the *'unacceptable language'* used after making it *'absolutely clear'* beforehand that he was to avoid discussing racial issues.

Hunter repeatedly used the n-word, including jokes about Liverpool player Luis Suarez who during the season had been accused of racially abusing Manchester United's Patric Evra. The incident came at the end of a season in which the PFA had been at the centre of other race storms involving John Terry, Ashley Cole, Anton Ferdinand and Rio Ferdinand. It is quite amazing that somebody, somewhere didn't think that inviting Mr Hunter might be left for another season or fifty!

The PFA insisted it had no inkling that the 44-year-old stand-up comic would use such language when they hired him for the event. *'He was booked on the basis of his recent television appearances,'* they said when the media storm broke around them. I can only assume that footballers are tucked up in bed between 9pm and 10pm on a Friday when Mr Hunter regularly appears on television

PFA chairman Clarke Carlisle added: *'In a conference call with Reginald and three members of The London Speakers Bureau, through which he was recruited, the makeup of our audience was outlined. It would be widely diverse including around 25 per cent of women and ages ranging from 18 to 80.'*.

'We made a really gross error of judgement in who we selected for our entertainment last night. I was embarrassed. I am probably going to get hung for it.'

I have had my own surreal moments. I gave a talk entitled *Life on a Local Newspaper* to one Probus club in Devon which was more humorous than serious. Before the meeting and over a coffee the chairman said they had a few items of business to conduct before he would call me. I sat on one side while the secretary read the minutes of the previous meeting which were like a scene from Dibley Parish Council. He spent 15 minutes explaining what had gone on at the last meeting including reference to the previous speaker who had *'enthralled and educated them'* on the subject of linear lettering and figures in the 19th century. When I eventually stood up to speak I apologised if the audience were expecting an intellectual talk, at which point a man on the front row said: *' He was bloody boring and we all feel asleep.'* I felt at home then.

Moments like that make public speaking memorable.

A talk I gave to a ladies' group nearly never happened when a church hall caretaker failed to open up the building one afternoon.

We stood out in the rain while the ladies group chairman telephoned his home. He obviously did not like to be disturbed because when he turned up with the keys he was in a foul mood and blamed his church committee for not keeping him informed. He grumbled and muttered and wanted everyone to know how badly he was treated until a very gentile old lady tugged him on the arm and said: ' *Tell me, which charm school did you graduate from?'* It stopped him in his tracks. When I came to speak I congratulated her and said she had achieved more in 10 seconds than I would probably achieve in 40 minutes. She nodded her agreement.

One golden rule for all speakers is never to lose your temper, no matter what the trying circumstances might be. This is sometimes easier said than done, particularly when some people will insist on talking while you are addressing them. It is bad manners, but the occasional culprit is generally too long in the tooth to change the habits of a lifetime. One of my pet hates is people who turn up late and refuse to enter the room quietly while I am speaking. I have only snapped once when giving a talk. A husband and wife duo banged the door behind them as they came in, made people stand up as they shuffled to the seats they wanted in the middle of a row and scraped their chairs as they put their coats on the back of their seats. I stopped in mid sentence, looked at them as they eventually sat down and asked: ' *Is there anything I can get you? Like a watch!'* The audience loved it and afterwards the chairman told me the couple behaved exactly the same way at most meetings.

It was not easy to keep my temper, however, in 2004 and 2005 when I forced a public referendum in Torbay on whether the area should have a directly elected mayor. There were so many dirty tricks being played by some councillors and their party apparatchiks that I had to be on my guard and careful what I said at the 16 public speaking engagements I undertook during the campaign – which was won by 3,000 votes. Different people were sent to the first six meetings by the town hall to either pour scorn on what I was saying by sitting in prominent positions, so the audience could see them shaking their heads and muttering denials, or to ask difficult questions prepared by council staff.

This continued for several weeks until at one well attended meeting in Babbacombe the councillor who had been sent along to cause as much mischief as possible dropped his list of questions on the floor. It was picked up by an alert local businessman who quickly realising what he had found proceeded to read out what had been written. After that I had no more trouble at any meeting I addressed.

My work has taken me round the world including three trips to the Falklands to train staff on both the local newspaper, the wonderfully named *Penguin News*, and the islands' radio station. On my third trip I had to give a 30 minute speech to the Falklands council about the work I was doing with both the journalists and members of a board of directors called The Media Trust and then repeat it on local radio for the 2,800 inhabitants. The Trust was made up of ordinary members of the public who acted as a watchdog on the newspaper and radio station and provided a buffer between government and media so there could be no accusations that the media were government controlled. It was an unusual speaking engagement, to say the least, to address a large audience without being able to see any of them!

I am sure there must have been times when some organisations thought about asking me to speak, but then thought better of it. The only time I have ever been told I was simply not wanted came when I was asked if I would be the external law advisor and speaker for Leeds University's media law courses. The invitation came via a friend at the Press Association who had the awkward job of telling me some months later; ' *You are the best qualified person in the country but they won't have you because you haven't got a degree*!' Apparently the aforementioned University of Life did not count!

I have rarely refused an invitation to speak unless it has clashed with my work, but one invitation in 2012 could have been fun, if I had gone ahead. Out of the blue Reading University sent me an email inviting me to address students on my 'exploits in space'. It said that if I could not travel to Reading personally they were prepared to arrange a video link. Some people might think I live on another planet, but I doubt whether they would want to hear about my experiences. The university had confused me with David Scott the American astronaut who was the first man to drive on the moon. I respectfully declined the invitation and while pointing out their mistake added that even my rendition of 'Fly me to the Moon' would not be worth hearing. I didn't get a response.

Nothing compares, however, with the story in 2013 of the talk on piracy given to Parkham WI in North Devon by ex-sea captain Colin Darch. As a former hostage of Somali pirates he was amazed to be greeted by a group of women wearing eye patches, wigs and fake wooden legs. Some of them brandished cutlasses.

The story of how he was beaten and held at gunpoint during a 47-day ordeal in the Indian Ocean in 2008 had obviously not reached the more rural parts of Devon. But Captain Darch reacted with good humour to the blunder and carried on his talk as planned.

'They seemed to be a little embarrassed but it didn't offend me in the slightest,' he told the Daily Mail from his home in Appledore, only a few miles from Parkham.

'The ladies didn't look the slightest bit like Somali pirates – more like the Pirates of Penzance. In the end they asked me to select the best costume. I gave them all marks out of ten. It was just a bit of fun.'

Captain Darch was held hostage by 20 gun-toting pirates after they leapt aboard his Danish ship, the Svitzer Korsakov, in the Gulf of Aden. Four Russian crew members were ordered to lie down on the deck but the captain and his Irish engineer, Fred Parle, 68, were needed to sail the 115ft vessel. He was struck over the head and warned he would be shot if his crew disobeyed their captors.

Six weeks later a rumoured £350,000 ransom was agreed and the crew were freed.

WI spokesman Stephanie George said: *'We didn't know much about him but the notes said he was Captain Darch and he was talking about piracy. I thought he was from a local fund-raising group who dress up as pirates to raise money for charity. Naturally everyone was aghast when we realised our mistake.*

'There he was delivering this harrowing story about how he was held hostage and feared for his life, and we were all sitting there dressed as Captain Hook. We apologised profusely but Mr Darch was a great sport and it didn't seem to faze him at all.

It is a priceless warning. Some groups never do any real research on who you are or what you will be really speaking to them about.

So I don't get caught out I now have a set of rules when it comes to public speaking I would recommend to everyone:

1. Prepare well and know your subject and audience. Don't think you can wing it on the night because unless you are a naturally gifted orator you will be a hopeless flop.

2. Arrive early rather than late – you can always sit in the car and put the radio on while you watch your audience arrive.

3. Never ever drink any alcohol when speaking to a luncheon or dinner group. You might think a couple of 'stiff ones' will calm your nerves, but they could mean disaster when you try to stand up and speak. You need a clear head.

4. Ensure you go to the room where you will be speaking to check the facilities before the allotted start time. Check the clip-on microphone switch, find out whether there is a table for you to place your notes and always have a glass of water handy in case that tickly cough returns.

5. Smile at your audience whenever you can and engage some eye contact. Most people want you to succeed, but they also want to be informed and entertained.

6. Carefully judge what jokes you tell with regard to taste.

7. Do not speak too fast and remember to pause every few minutes.

8. Do not walk around too much.

9. Do not fiddle with coins in your pockets or any other items.

10. Make sure you go to the toilet beforehand.

11. Try and change the tone of your voice throughout your speech, either to highlight a key point or wake up your audience!

One public speaking role I have never enjoyed is that of best man at a wedding. At the last count I had performed this function on nine occasions in addition to giving the main speech at both my daughter's and eldest son's weddings. I have heard enough awful, cringing best man speeches to know that while it is regarded as a necessary duty, the audience simply want you to get up, say a few original friendly words, propose the appropriate toast and sit down.

Ten minutes is the absolute maximum for any best man's speech and it is best if you remember that the bride and groom's aunts, uncles and possibly grandparents are listening to your every word. Stag night revelations are not required, nor details of schoolboy pranks. Any mention of previous girlfriends and their sexual prowess are totally taboo.

Yet time and time again I have had to sit through badly presented, sometimes totally boring, often offensive and crude speeches that would have benefited from someone using the old fashioned hook to drag the best man away.

A couple of politically correct jokes are fine. Words that spell out what a wonderful couple they are go down well with the families. A bowl full of ' thank yous' are also necessary. After that sit down. Good wedding speeches should be like a mini skirt – short enough to attract attention; long enough to cover the bare essentials.

The only mischief I ever got up to at a wedding was as an usher when the best man wanted to play a prank. The bride's parents were teetotal Methodists so there was no alcohol available at the reception. The best man and I knew that both the bride and groom frequented local pubs so we wrote out six fictitious cards from the Dog and Duck, Queen's Head etc, slipped them into the pile on the top table and he read them out during his speech. The bride's mother was furious and when the meal was over gave us a piece of her mind.

One wedding my wife and I were glad we were not invited to involved a friend who got married 'on the rebound'. One minute she was engaged to the love of her life, the next it was all off and she was going out with somebody else. Within a few months a wedding was back on to the new man in her life. At the reception her father referred to the former boyfriend as his daughter's husband rather than the groom, much to everyone's embarrassment.

Apart from my schooldays, I can only remember having to sit through two very, very boring speeches, both of which I was surprisingly looking forward to. The first was given by the then Foreign Secretary Douglas Hurd at an editors' conference in Birmingham. Mr Hurd was a popular MP and Minister but as far as I was concerned he could bore for England. His 45-minute monotone offering was the last thing a group of editors wanted to hear when the bar was still open. Fortunately the night was saved when I came to leave and literally bumped into Sir Stanley Matthews who had been the speaker in another room. We exchanged apologies. I would have much preferred to have heard Sir Stanley speak about his footballing days.

Another sporting hero was Sir Garfield Sobers, the great West Indian cricketer. I went to watch him tear England apart in several 1970s Test matches and also when he played county cricket. Thirty years later he spoke without notes at a Paignton Cricket Club dinner and fund-raiser at Torquay's Riviera Centre and rambled all over the place. It was quite embarrassing as he repeated himself several times and lost his way. Good fortune came to my aid that night because I won £250 in the raffle!

At least Mr Hurd and Mr Sobers did not resort to telling smutty jokes to entertain their audience. Nowadays too many after-dinner speakers liberally sprinkle dirty jokes and bad language into their offering. They believe every sentence should include the 'f' word and other obscenities which they pepper throughout their boring, repetitive discourse. They call it entertainment but only those who have had too much to drink think it entertaining – the rest find it offensive and cringe-making.

Innuendo is fine. A master of that is comedian Don Mclean whom I got to know and befriend during my time in Birmingham. He has retained the art of holding his audience's attention without resorting to the use of one bad or offensive word. It's a skill I admire.

Sadly, I cannot think of any modern politician or sportsman I feel I simply have to listen to if the opportunity arises. In most cases you can predict much of what they are going to say in advance, their efforts dulled by their attempts to survive in a media world where sound bites are needed for television in particular.

Thankfully there are people who can enthral an audience at a purely local level and they are in great demand by the hundreds of organisations which meet every week up and down the country in village halls, pubs and hotels. In the following chapters some of them share their experiences.

I was once asked to name the three people I would have most liked to have heard give a speech and I had no hesitation in naming David Lloyd George, the Welsh windbag to his opponents, Billy Graham in his hey-day and Moses.

There was much to dislike about Lloyd George, but having read his memoirs and several books about his life and times there can be little doubt he was a spellbinding speaker who at his peak held an audience in the palm of his hand. Can you say that about any British politician today?

From the people I have spoken to who attended one of Billy Graham's Crusades I have no doubt he was a magnificent speaker who touched the hearts and souls of those who heard him – a special gift he used to the best of his ability.

As for Moses, well anyone who at the age of 80 could lead hundreds of thousands of people for the next 40 years through a desert to their promised land must have been a gifted speaker as well as a man of action. From accounts in the Bible he had to deliver many strong speeches to keep his flock moving in the right direction.

CHAPTER TWO

THE EDITORS

You cannot hope to bribe or twist, Thank God! The British journalist. But, see what the man will do unbribed, There's no occasion to. - Humbert Wolfe

Dave King, former editor of the Swindon Advertiser, had to endure a formidable challenge before he got to speak to the ladies of the WI in Hampshire. He recalls his ordeal.

I've had the privilege to give many talks to schools, business groups, the likes of Rotary, and the good old Women's Institute.

When I had just finished my challenge of running around the British Isles in 2007, and was in the midst of writing a book to accompany the charity venture, it was agreed by myself and the autism charity that we should organise a series of talks to promote the book and the charity. This included facing the fearsome band of folk from the Women's Institutes in front of whom I had to audition X-Factor style. It was one of my toughest challenges ever.

This was the same trusted organisation of fearsome ladies who once gave Tony Blair a torrid time at their national conference a few years back.

Every year the Hampshire WI hold auditions for speakers wanting to talk to their members around the county. You could describe it as the WI does X-Factor. I even had to pay a fee for the privilege of attending the audition and then £10 for an entry in the WI handbook if successful. Fellow WI members were invited to attend the audition I was invited to undergo and for this outing 43 ladies turned up at the WI headquarters in Winchester to hear four speakers talk on a variety of subjects from press photography and the world of gastronomic delights, to adventures in Borneo and my subject...autism and running.

I was there with Sally from the Hampshire Autistic Society. We were greeted by a lovely lady called Cherry and offered tea and small talk, I was 'bricking it'. So too was Sally who admitted later that if we could have made a dignified exit then she would have – and I would have joined her. We could hear the laughter from upstairs where the Fleet Street photographer was in full swing. We didn't have too many laughs in our half-hour ditty.

At the appointed hour, a petite, silver-haired lady called Fearne met us and led us into the room where the fearsome-looking 43 ladies greeted us. It was intimidating. We had five minutes to set up, so Sally and I busied ourselves putting up a display, plugging in a computer and a projector for a five-minute film which we wanted to show at the end.

I am never normally edgy with public speaking, but it was the sight of those ladies clutching their pads of paper and pens and the fact they were judging us which was unnerving. They were no Simon Cowell, but this was so bizarre. When the lady in front row started scribbling some notes within seconds of Sally talking I thought "uh oh, we're dead in the water!"

In truth the talk went well as the ladies warmed to us. We got a few laughs; we also got some tears at the end from the video which I had put together with a friend from the BBC telling the story of autism through the eyes of Ross. It was an exhausting half hour, I was sweating badly by the time we left the room to make way for the talk from the flame-haired speaker about life in Borneo.

How did we do? Well, amazingly we got accepted.

Bob Satchwell is Executive Director of the Society of Editors and a former editor of the Cambridge Evening News. He explains how to adlib when you realise without warning you are expected to be the star performer

It was a routine autumn evening out for the editor of a regional evening paper - an annual dinner at the Farmers' Club. This time it was the regional branch of the association of land agents and valuers (forgive me if I forget the precise name I usually think of it as the wheel tappers and shunters club).

Given the venue and the all-male audience consisting of landowners who used the services of the organisation to set rents, farmers who had to pay them plus a motley collection of fellow travellers, it was set to be an interesting evening where ale flowed before a dinner of best roast beef with all the trimmings washed down with copious quantities of an acceptable red wine.

The pre dinner beer reception seemed to last forever, so much so that I was ready for some blotting paper long before we sat down to eat.

I was ushered to the top table to be seated between the regional president and the local secretary. I devoured a sizable plateful of beef while enjoying pleasant and, yes, interesting, conversation about the value of various types of land, whether the winter wheat was all in yet and the price and benefits of straw versus shredded newspapers for horses' bedding.

The wine flowed and the farmers sent for second helpings before a bowlful of apple crumble and custard arrived. While summoning the strength to punish my stomach further and thinking how I might be able to find an excuse to leave early before the after dinner drinking started in earnest, I enquired gently of my neighbour about the format for the evening.

The secretary explained: "*The president speaks first to welcome you and the national president. The national president then praises the work of regional members and tells us just how important we are to the British way of life. He's always the warm up for the guest speaker, the entertainment - the guest speaker who gets a long introduction from the regional president.*"

"*And who might the "entertainment be*" I asked nonchalantly . . . and you've guessed it . . . "*Why you of course, didn't you know?*" came the deafening reply.

Trying not to panic and thanking God that a comfort break was being announced I made a quick exit from the table to gather some inspiration. Little chance of that as I seemed to know everyone there including estate agents who were the downmarket partners of the land valuers as well as being important advertisers who required regular doses of ego polish.

I returned empty headed to the table just in time for the president to start proceedings. I searched my pockets for paper and pen, finding only the invitation to the do. I was revitalised by the discovery that it was not my secretary who had forgotten to warn me that I was supposed to speak (and therefore not drink beforehand). The invitation seemed to suggest they just wanted to entertain me - no mention of wanting me to be "*the entertainment*" as the secretary put it.

So while the national president's monologue continued for what seemed nowhere long enough for my purposes, I pretended to be making notes from his erudite remarks while in reality I was scribbling down punch lines of stories that with luck this lot might not have heard - or at least would not remember - and jotting down names of some in the audience who I could gently insult for comic effect on the grounds that they would be pleased to be recognised.

The national president sat down to a bare ripple of applause to be replaced by the regional president who thankfully read out the whole of my CV providing precious extra minutes for me to ask for a foaming pint of beer to wash down the port that had appeared with the cheese course (that remained untouched in my case).

The foaming pint was a vital prop. As the welcoming titter of applause faded, I took a slug from it and expressed a hope that the beer would keep flowing. The audience needed little urging and the distraction of ordering and being served full glasses thus earned me goodwill and drew attention away from my ill prepared contribution to the evening.

Clearly the beer worked. I sat down after ten minutes to thunderous applause as the audience breathed a sigh of relief that they could rush to the gents.

I even received a very pleasant letter of thanks.

And that reminds me of another occasion when ad libbing was seriously required.

The organisers of the regular sportsmen's dinners had a really bright idea.

The quarterly events were strictly male and consisted mainly of retired sports stars or football managers effing and blinding their way through mildly amusing reminiscences that the flow of booze turned into hilarious if semi pornographic and definitely sexist entertainment.

Given that background the "bright idea" seemed like an oxymoron. They would hold a Sportsman's Dinner *Ladies* Night.

The women clearly had no idea because they seemed keen to find out how their menfolk spent their evenings compiling massive hangovers. Afterwards they were genuinely surprised that men found such a well-behaved evening so enchanting.

They were even flattered by a formal toast to the ladies in which, especially as my wife was by my side, I laid on the old fashioned charm with the aid of a JCB.

What they didn't know was that the retired sports star had to cut whole sections from his speech. You could almost hear the bleeps as he stuttered through the gaps.

Even worse was the plight of the wretched comedian who had been booked for a Sportsman's Dinner . . . with no mention of the ladies.

He sat next to me on the top table without any of the fine food or drink passing his lips as we - the comedian, my wife and I - tried to provide him with some vaguely acceptable stories to replace the distinctly blue jokes which was his usual, and only, repertoire. We even managed to re-write a couple of his offerings to make them vaguely acceptable - just.

And there was the time I once had to address a year group at one of my daughters' schools. One bright spark asked the best question: *"How much do you earn?* The only response to the smart ass was: *"Not nearly enough to keep my daughter in pocket money."* She was sitting next to the questioner.

Ian Murray, editor of the Southampton Echo, recalls one memorable trip to give a talk.

My favourite moment from giving talks on my life as a journalist came a couple of years ago here in Southampton when I accepted an invitation to speak to a women's luncheon group at a parish hall.

The date was put in the diary some months prior, and on the day I set off in plenty of time. As often with these local talks I carried with me in the car boot the precious first ever edition of the Southern Echo – August 20 1888. I hadn't travelled far when I spotted smoke coming from the rear of the car in my mirror, pulled up at the side of the road and leapt for safety. Standing at the road side contemplating what to do I realised I had left the precious volume in the boot and, braving the flames now licking the underside of the car, dashed back, wrenched open the boot and dragged the huge broadsheet-size bound copies clear.

Next problem was what to do with my speaking engagement. I had visions of the ladies fretting over my non arrival. I didn't want to let them down after the engagement had been booked for so long. I phoned the office, asked them to send around someone from the garage to deal with the car which had thankfully now stopped smoking, and someone from the newsroom to take me to the parish hall. I was scooped up by a photographer who deposited me at the parish hall car park just ten minutes late.

Looking a little dishevelled, red of face, wreaking of smoke, and struggling with the huge old bound file, I burst into the hall making loud apologies from behind the book. The response was silence. I apologised again, putting the book down, to be met by more puzzled expressions. *"it's good of you to apologise,"* came a voice from the stage, *" but we were actually expecting you next month. Our speaker for today has already started."*

At that I was politely shown the door to wait on the car park for the photographer to be found to return and pick me up. It soon started raining.

Bob Bounds, Editor of the Medway Messenger, likes to tell as many local stories as possible to his audiences when invited to speak. Here are a couple of his favourites.

A colleague who was working on the now-defunct East Kent Times was told to cover a story about a chap from Broadstairs who hit a bit of minor fame in showbiz circles and had started dating the actress Lesley Ann Down.

The reporter went around to his mother's house and, invited in, asked where they had met. The woman replied, "*at a party thrown by Ava Gardner*". To which the reporter said:"*Oh, is she from Broadstairs too?*"

I gave a talk to a group of primary school pupils and went on about the job and newspapers etc and when they looked suitably bored asked if there were any questions. One lad, about six years old, thrust his arm up and said: "*why does the Sun put ladies' boobs on page 3?*" (cue one speechless editor).

The best one-liner I've ever heard came when as a young reporter I was sent to cover the monthly meeting of the Maidstone Chamber of Commerce. It was a warm evening, all the 'suits' were sat down when a glamorous businesswoman arrived just as the meeting was about to start. Eyeing the lascivious looks from her male colleagues she said: "*Ooh it's hot in here, maybe I should take my top off*". to which the chairman said: "*I'm afraid we'll have to take that under matters arising*"...

Danny Lockwood is the owner and publisher of The Press a weekly in the Dewsbury/Batley area, League Weekly, a rugby league newspaper, and Yorkshire Golfer. He recalls what it is like to 'die on stage'.

Apart from my many and varied ventures as an editor, publisher and now author (my book The Islamic Republic of Dewsbury) I've also done public speaking in various guises. In 1987 I was doing my after-match bit as captain of the Belmont Shore rugby union team in Long Beach, California. We'd just played the crew from the Royal Yacht Britannia actually.

I got a few laughs and afterwards a bloke approached me and asked me if I'd ever done stand-up. I said no. A few days later I was at The Improv comedy club on Melrose Avenue in Hollywood, with the owner Budd Friedman, Rodney Dangerfield etc. The following Sunday night at 9pm I was onstage, cheered on by a gang of friends who'd driven up and paid good dollars to watch.

You know the legendary 'hook' with which failing acts are dragged by the neck from the stage? It isn't a hook, it's a bloke with a torch at the back of the room who flashes it. Five minutes after going on I was skulking off. I had died a death. Five minutes after that I was sitting on the sidewalk outside a 7-eleven chugging a bottle of Old English 800, a cheap but strong malt liquor. A police car stopped, thinking I was a vagrant and moved me on.

That was the last of the comedy.

I had a brief career as resident 'emcee' at the Westin Bonaventure hotel in LA, the highlight being co-hosting a televised 1988 Olympic Games event with Jon Voight. It went downhill though and my next gig was 'co-hosting' with Spuds McKenzie the dog from Budweiser Lights' television adverts; it was a disaster thanks to the bull terrier repeatedly suffering from a weak bladder in the hotel atrium.

Shortly after that I 'emceed' a televised beauty pageant and the electrician hadn't wired the stage mic properly. While interviewing the delectable Miss Maywood, one Sandy Rivera, I must have licked my dry lips because my tongue touched the mic – which really was 'live' - and the shock sent me hurtling backwards through the garland archway, to land in a heap in the backstage curtains. Despite dishevelled semi-paralysis down one side of my face, and holding a microphone like it was a spitting cobra, I did get through the evening.

Sandy Rivera came third and somehow resisted my ministrations to leave that evening in a fast car for a wild weekend in Mexico. I went anyway.

That was the end of my stage career – it was back to newspapers and magazines. I now own/publish The Press a weekly in the Dewsbury/Batley area, League Weekly, a rugby league newspaper, and Yorkshire Golfer, a monthly. Libel writs have nothing on public speaking.

Rachael Campey, former editor of the Yorkshire Post, found out exactly what upsets readers when she gave her first talk.

My first public speaking experience came not long after I had been promoted to Assistant Editor at the Northern Echo. I was feeling very pleased with myself and having just spent a few years on news desk felt I knew what made the paper tick. I had never done any public speaking before and I was told (not asked) the day before the engagement to go along to a working men's club in County Durham to talk for a few minutes "*about the paper*" to a small lunch time audience.

I was the post lunch guest...."*Nothing at all to be worried about,*" said the Editor: "*You'll be fine. Nothing to it....*"

I hastily put together a few notes about the history of the paper and new developments in the future. I arrived and made my way through the bar. A hum of conversation, the "chock" of snooker balls hitting pockets, and beer glasses clinking..... A few cursory glances in my direction as I was taken through to the next room where I was to speak. Only it wasn't a room - it was a barn of a place. A huge hall filled with rows of people who turned to look at me as I was guided the length of the hall and up on to a platform. All I could see was a sea of faces. And all I could hear were the snooker balls firing into pockets....and the words of the Editor *"You'll be fine....nothing to it."*

I spoke for about 20 minutes, burbling on about the paper's proud history, the stories we'd covered, the bright future - colour presses, new technology. All very earnest, enthusiastic - and naive, really!

Polite applause. Then QUESTIONS.

I remember it well. The first came from the back of the hall. Well, it started there. The gentleman got up out of his seat and walked half way up the hall and looked up at my flustered face.

"Well, lass, that was all very well but I have just one question: When the bloody hell are you going to get the crosswords right?!"

"Crosswords?" I mumbled, confused and not immediately grasping the importance or, indeed, the necessity for the question. What the hell had crosswords got to do with important things like page leads??

Everything it turned out. Because after my interrogator went on to explain that the last edition had failed to give the answer to the previous day's clue to three down,(*"and this happens all the time"* he added....All hell let loose.

Suddenly hands across the audience dived into pockets and handbags, and then a rustling sound wafted through the air. Nearly everyone had come with CUTTINGS - some going back years - and which were now being waved in front of me. More crosswords with the wrong or no answers; headlines with words spelt incorrectly; weather reports with the wrong tide times; wrong captions, wrong names.....and stories that people felt were insensitive, badly researched or carelessly written.

41

Welcome to the real world, Rachael. Welcome to what really matters to readers.

As experiences go, that day was unforgettable and had an enormous impact on me. There wasn't a single angry voice in the audience, but it was - for them - a long-awaited opportunity to tell the young whipper-snapper from the Northern Echo a few facts of life. The dawning of a bright, technologically-advanced, new age could wait for a few important basics. I answered questions throughout the afternoon - or rather I fielded them - as I collected more and more cuttings.

None of the errors it seemed had diminished their loyalty to the paper, but they lived in hope that the people who congratulated themselves on producing a *"great"* newspaper would realise that it wasn't worth the paper it was written on if you couldn't *"get the crosswords right."*

I should also add that while I felt like decapitating the Editor with a snooker cue on my return to the office, he knew what he was doing when he sent me there.

When I became editor of the Express&Echo in Exeter, which was my first editorship, I did a lot of public speaking at community groups, schools, village halls and at the University of Exeter.

I was very busy and sometimes preparing a speech got knocked down the list of priorities. Like the time I gave my first public speech at the University. It had been a busy day and I'd left myself no time to research and prepare. I knew it was a school prize-giving ceremony but I had no idea about the scale of the event or size of the audience. Basics, really.

I scribbled a few notes on the back of an envelope and rushed to the campus. I was late and was met at reception and ushered into......the Great Hall. There were hundreds of people in the room: parents, pupils, teaching staff. And there was an upper tier, also packed.

My jaw dropped. I was completely overwhelmed. I was so shocked by the size of the audience and the venue, that it felt like I was having an out-of-body experience and I was somewhere on that upper tier watching myself being led into the unknown.

I genuinely thought it would be a small, intimate affair and I had totally misjudged the size and status of the event.

Fortunately there were platform speeches and introductions before I needed to get up. I glanced around the hall and looked at the faces of the students and their parents. I had my scribbled notes in front of me which I realised were hopelessly inadequate. I quickly took out some spare note cards and wrote some new words which I have kept to this day: memories of my first secondary school speech day and how I went there with my hair in bunches, with one bunch shorter than the other as I had burnt it off in the bunsen burner the previous day.

I wrote down the quote from James Cameron's wonderful book about his life as a newspaper reporter and broadcaster: -Point of Departure. "*Hope subsides, but curiosity remains. Every day is, necessarily, and even now, a point of departure. We shall see...*"

Then I wrote down "*why journalism...and how did I get here!*"...I jotted down a few words about my work experience - hospital porter, nursing auxiliary and journalistic career path - and then at the end I wrote: " *you don't have to be a journalist to be curious....have fun, don't be bland...go for it....strive, learn to cope, each day a point of departure....*".

I should have added" *Don't panic*!

I think back now to that day and how the experience could so easily have turned into a nightmare for me - and the audience.

But, actually, it was the audience that saved me. Especially the students' faces. I could remember me in that same situation years before. Memories and experiences flooded back and I gave my entire speech without looking at a note. Out of sheer terror came a connection.

God knows how that happened but the applause afterwards was like nothing I'd ever had before. A genuinely enthusiastic response with a forest of people waiting to talk to me later.

I am not saying: don't be prepared. I never got into that predicament again, but finding a connection - even a few minutes before you stand up - is vital. It saved my life that day!!

Good old James Cameron. He wrote about the "*agonising narrow line between sincerity and technique, between the imperative and the glib - so fine and delicate a boundary that one frequently misses it altogether...*"

That day I'd stupidly left no time for technique; all that was left was to reach for sincerity.

Spencer Feeney, former editor of the Swansea Evening Post, remembers two stories he used to tell when giving talks during his editorship. They illustrate that a sports reporter's life is not as glamorous as it may appear.

The first concerns a sports reporter called Jim Hill. He was for many years the Daily Express's man in South Wales. Jim was in Australia, covering the Welsh rugby team's tour of that country. This was before modern satellite phone communications, when reporters would sit in hotel rooms for hours waiting for operators in far distant lands to make their connection. Jim had patiently waited for a line from Sydney to London. Eventually the London operator's ghostly voice came faintly down the line to his hotel room. There was another lengthy wait while the operator put him through to the Daily Express switchboard. Another delay before the switchboard put him through to the sports desk. At last a voice barked: "*Sports Desk! What do you want?*"

Jim was about to say "*Jim Hill in Sydney here*" but did not get further than announcing his name before the harassed sub-editor on the other end interrupted: "*Jim Hill? He's in Australia!*" And put the phone down.

The second story concerns Clem Thomas, former Wales rugby international, businessman, and doyen of rugby writers during his years covering the sport for The Observer. Clem joined the rest of the Welsh sports press pack on a wild West Wales Saturday to cover a Welsh Cup-tie between Laugharne, the village made famous by Dylan Thomas but also well-known locally for having a rugby team of tough farmers and lobster fishermen, and the aristocrats of Swansea.

It was a typically fractious occasion as the junior side attempted to bridge the gulf in ability by ferociously tackling every Swansea player with faint regard to such niceties as whether they were anywhere near the ball at the time.

It was the final minutes, and Swansea were clinging on to a narrow lead. The ball was punted high into the lead-grey sky. All eyes followed it. Suddenly there was a crack, suspiciously like the sound of fist connecting with upturned jaw. The Laugharne captain lay flat on his back. Near him was a Swansea player looking as inconspicuous as is possible when you are six feet six inches tall with badly grazed knuckles on your right hand.

The sound of outrage rumbled from the crowd like thunder on Cardigan Bay. The referee took one look, blew the final whistle and ran for the safety of the dressing room, closely followed (in order) by the Swansea team, the press pack, and a large part of the male population of Laugharne fuelled on a mixture of indignation and Felinfoel Double Dragon Ale.

The ref bolted himself in one room. The Swansea team locked themselves away in their changing room. The press pack sent for beer and sandwiches and settled down for the siege. The crowd started to dismantle the clubhouse in their enthusiasm to get their hands on anyone wearing a Swansea shirt.

And then, amid this chaos, came the refined tones of Clem, who had started composing his match report. "*I say chaps. How do you spell magnanimous?*"

Colin Davison, former editor of the Western Morning News and other titles, reveals how humbling it can be when giving any talk and the soul destroying experience of speaking to an audience of three.

In 2011 I had a biography published, *Through the Magic Door,* and travelled all over the country, responding to invitations to talk about its subject, the children's writer Ursula Moray Williams. The appearances were almost invariably unpaid, but often, at the end of a 45-minute presentation, and before I set off on another 80-mile journey to get home, the host chairman would ask about the price or other publishing details. I'd look hopefully toward the audience of 30 or 40 women and be told: "*The good news is we always buy a copy of a book from our speaker - so we can lend it out to all the members.*" Nett author receipts per copy, approximately £1.50.

That was at least one of the productive visits. Another chairman checked to ensure she had the correct title and name of the publisher. "*I must get it next week*," she said, encouragingly. "*The mobile library comes on Wednesday.*"

Thank goodness for those WI and women's groups meetings who would always welcome a speaker, any speaker, provided they came cheaply, or in the case of local editors entirely free. As well as having the opportunity to praise one's own newspaper to the skies, remind the audience of the nobility of the journalistic profession, and bask in a comforting self-delusion of one's importance, one was often greeted with old fashioned tea and scones, applauded <u>before</u> saying a word, and invited to participate fully in the other activities of the meeting. This often included judging competitions, typically featuring royal celebrations immortalised on paper doylies or tea-pot covers, and knickers decorated for St George's Day - the winner on one occasion being mostly conveniently XXL and able to accommodate a splendid St George erect recto with the Dragon couchant verso.

The trickiest moment came, however, after being invited to stay to listen to an illustrated talk on breast cancer. At the end, a false breast was handed around for the otherwise entirely female audience to fondle and compare with the real thing. I declined to express a particular preference.

Other disasters included going to present an illustrated talk about newspaper photographs, that depended entirely on a series of slides. On arriving at the venue, the group announced that unfortunately their projector wasn't working, so could I give the talk without it?

On another occasion I was invited to address a local history society about my newspaper and discovered there were only three members of the audience. The host nevertheless carried on regardless, and introduced me to the audience without a flicker, so naturally I ploughed on, occasionally even addressing the empty seats all around the hall as much to spare her embarrassment as mine. Despite having a rather limited audience on which to concentrate my best lines, I failed nevertheless to retain the interest of all, as was clearly indicated by the closed eyes and heavy breathing of my host's neighbour. That I was still able to carry on was largely due to the final member of the audience, a young lady avidly taking notes.

It was some small consolation that my thoughts and anecdotes about the job of a local newspaper editor were of sufficient interest for her to record. Perhaps she would go home to share these pearls of wisdom with her family, tell my gags to her friends, saying what a marvellous, fascinating man she had heard at the society. *So it hadn't been such a bad evening, after all, I told the paper's news editor the following day.* "Ah," piped up his assistant, "*you would have met our new village correspondent. I said you were going, so told her she'd better go along to take notes.*" Sic transit gloria.'

Derby Telegraph editor Neil White is an avid Coventry City fan. When the club moved out of Coventry's Ricoh Stadium in 2013 and played their 'home' games at Northampton's ground he was asked to speak at a fan's protest rally. His lack of preparation nearly let him down.

My most memorable act of public speaking did emphasise that new technology aids might not be that helpful when taking to the stage.

Seven thousand people marched through the streets of the Coventry and I was asked to be one of the speakers - not the editor of the Coventry Telegraph - when it reached the city centre.

Anyway, I had thought I could wing it until I reached the meeting point and realised just how many people were going to be there. Thus, I reached for my iphone and in the space of 20 minutes crafted what I thought were inspirational words to inspire the faithful.

The march all went rather well with a truly fantastic atmosphere. After a prominent Coventry MP did his spiel, I was called to the stage with iphone with notes ready in hand.

I shouted out the words *"I love Coventry City"* and the thousands broke out into huge cheers and applause. I looked up and there among the crowd were my mum, dad, wife and many friends..

And then I looked back down to my iphone and it had gone blank ...

A gap of what was probably just three seconds seemed like an hour before I realised that I couldn't stand there, put in my password and wait for the notes to reappear so I did what I had planned all along...and winged it.

Fortunately for Neil he has rarely been called upon to give a humorous talk. *'I have an absolutely appalling memory for jokes etc. This is something of a problem when one considers that, aside of public speaking, I've been best man four times,'* he says.

Brendan Hanrahan, former editor of the Torquay Herald Express and Clacton Gazette, remembers a time when he was deputy editor of the South Wales Evening Post.

The "funniest", most awkward or memorable incident regarding public speaking happened to me in Swansea. In 1998-99 I was part of the four-strong organising committee (the others were Dave

Woolley and Sean McKear from Swansea Council and local bookshop owner and Dylan 'nut' Jeff Towns) of the city's first Dylan Thomas Festival in my role as Deputy Editor of the Post. The opening night and reception approached at which, among others, two of the poet's children, Bronwy and Llewellyn, were present along with the alleged great and the good etc. For some reason, I was asked, or rather, chosen to be the only person to read a piece of Dylan's actual work as the last speaker.

Things didn't start well when I walked into the Dylan Thomas Centre that Friday evening to hear the great man's voice itself booming out like God audibly, but not too loud, on tape as he read some of his own various works of genius.

Oh, dear, I thought, what will an Irish Brummie sound like compared to that voice? I kept checking my pockets in my favourite grey-blue check suit to ensure I had Thomas's book of Collected Poems in my pocket (my own copy I should add - I was and still am a DT nut).

As I was meeting and greeting people, it was also useful that I had got into the habit of carrying lots of my business cards in all my suit(s) pockets.

Anyway, my turn duly approached to conclude the speaking and I began by saying how humbled I felt by the honour of being asked to read a piece of Dylan's works. Automatically, I reached to my right suit pocket to check the book was there and lifted it out. I pulled it out with such gusto (or nervousness) that all the business cards flew out of the pocket like a flock of pigeons coming out of a loft.

Undeterred, I proceeded unintentionally to repeat the trick when I moved the book to my left pocket before I wrenched it out again. In a picture taken - its current place unknown - I looked like I had been showered with large confetti around me on the floor.

I've never forgotten it and I hope Dylan would have thought it apt given his reputation. The poem I chose was "In My Craft Or Sullen Art". I was sullen for a while, but the audience didn't seem to mind.

Vivien Meath, former editor of the Clitheroe Advertiser, and the reporter who took over from me in Barnoldswick when I moved into sports reporting, has entertained many people with her witty talks about local newspapers. Here she recalls some of the joys and less happy occasions.

At the end of my talk to the village Monday Club, I was thanked profusely by the secretary who announced: *"Today's guest speaker will go down in history. No one fell asleep!"*

I later discovered that several of the members regularly 'nodded off' within minutes of the meeting starting. Praise indeed!

During my career as a news editor, then editor in the Ribble Valley, I regularly accepted invitations to speak to various organisations. The fee was never great and regularly donated back to a local charity supported by the newspaper.

In retirement my fee stayed the same, sufficient to cover travelling costs and a little extra to warrant giving an evening up. One talk led to another and, days after giving a successful talk to a packed meeting of business people in Skipton, I found myself in front of a handful of people at a local church in my home town.

I had altered the talk to include local eccentric personalities from my time as a trainee reporter in the late 1960s. Arriving I was greeted by two rows of seats - virtually all empty. Waiting to see if anyone was going to turn out, I was put well and truly in my place by a lady wielding a huge empty teapot. *"I don't know if you're usually paid, but we don't pay speakers here. We haven't enough money."*

A few people wandered in and, as I began, I realised that not only was the church membership in decline, but those present were 'offcomers' and had no interest at all in the town's past. Not a smile, not a titter, no questions - no one fell asleep - but after a long hour, I thanked my hosts - and left."

Steve White was Editor of the Wiltshire Times and then Deputy Editor of the Western Daily Press for nine years before leading a team of Press Association sub-editors and designers producing pages for the Daily Mirror, Sunday Mirror and Sunday People. In September 2013 he was appointed PA's Editor, Trinity Mirror Production, which meant he also took responsibility for the team of sub-editors and designers producing pages for the Glasgow-based Daily Record and Sunday Mail, but when it came to public speaking he found it much harder work.

As editor of the Wiltshire Times I was regularly called upon to speak in public.

Although my heart sank every time I opened these invitations I regarded them as unmissable opportunities to promote the paper, explain what we were trying to achieve and demonstrate why more people should buy "us".

While never enjoying the prospect, and always feeling nervous as the occasion approached, these events invariably went well - despite the South West audiences no doubt sometimes struggling with my Yorkshire mumblings.

Although speaking in public does get easier the more you do it, I always felt happier tackling questions and answers sessions. I believed I could give a better, more natural, account of myself and the paper when answering specific questions rather than delivering a prepared speech.

Looking back on it, perhaps all I needed was a better scriptwriter.

Jon Grubb, former editor of the Lincolnshire Echo, on the art of judging an audience

I was working at the Nottingham Post and was asked to give a talk at a dinner for North Notts Magistrates. I assumed they would be a fairly stiff brigade and produced a fairly dry speech but added in a couple of risqué jokes with the intention of editing them out when I had judged the audience.

When I arrived they were indeed a very conservative looking bunch and I resolved to use the "clean" version of the speech.

As it turned out I used the wrong one and once I realised what I had done it was too late so I used the jokes whilst cringing inside - ready for the stony silence and disapproving looks.

As it was the jokes went down a storm and most of the comments I had afterwards were that they'd wished I had used more.

It taught me fairly early in my "management career" that you indeed never should judge a book by its cover.

Jim Parker, editor of the Torquay Herald Express, revealed more than he wanted to when addressing a group of leading businessmen and women.

I launched our Business Excellence Awards one year at a very early business breakfast meeting in front of leading members of the business fraternity and alongside the then mayor and South Devon's College principal(OBE).

It was one of my first public speaking engagements and got in my car pleased that I had got through it – only to then discover that my flies had been open during the entire event!

At another business awards event in front of 200 people I was talking about the importance and need of a bypass to transform South Devon's fortunes. I said we needed the support of government and friendly ministers and for some inexplicable reason gave a big wink to then minister Ben Bradshaw who was our VIP guest sitting in the audience. It must have worked because we are now in the middle of the bypass being built.

I was asked to be the guest speaker at a club for retired businessmen. I thought I was doing pretty well talking about a variety of stories in which I had been involved including IRA bomb cells in a Torquay hotel, interviewing Great Train robber Ronnie Biggs, the day the Mafia were in town as well as 'routine' murders and the evening I was called by the police to help end a siege – then I realised two members of the audience were dozing peacefully in the front row.

And then there was the time I co-hosted one of our annual Sports Awards finals nights in front of 300 people. I was asked to 'big up' the most important and final award of the night – Sports Personality of the Year. I did with a *'and now to our final and most prestigious award of the night. The winner is ...* ' and I went on to extol his virtues only to have to tell the audience he was outside having a fag!

Lisa Watson is editor of one of my favourite newspapers – the wonderfully named Penguin News which serves the Falkland Islands and has a near 100% readership. Like many of us, she was not prepared for the questions she had to field from local children.

I really haven't done a lot of public speaking, although obviously I've done a ton of interviews with the British and foreign press.

But I did give a talk to a large group of infant school children last year - it was about my book 'Waking up to war' which I wrote for children about my experiences in 1982. The teachers had been reading it to the children as part of the 30th anniversary of the War.

The staff also invited me to take along two of my favourite childhood books in order that I could chat about them to the kiddies. I took Black Beauty and Heidi along. My talk had gone very well and the children seemed very interested until I mentioned my favourite books. At this point, the little boy sat on the floor next to my knee tapped me gently on the leg and when I looked down I saw a pair of large brown very concerned eyes.

When I asked him if he was OK. He pointed at 'Heidi' with its very girly cover and said: "*You're not going to read us that damn thing are you?*" I could only laugh and promise him I wouldn't inflict it on him. He was the cutest little thing and peppered me with questions throughout the entire talk.

Andy Cooper is editor in chief of Devon Life and is the former editorial director of Cornwall and Devon Media which includes some of the largest weekly papers in the country.

Before Christmas 2013 I was asked to read a lesson at Wells Cathedral as we were sponsoring the event. It was a very 'High Church' event and, as each speaker was due on, a very haughty robed official came to collect you from the congregation.

My turn duly came and I was 'collected'. While we were waiting for the music to die down so I could read my lesson, the official said to me: "*I expect you've spoken in front of large audiences before, but there is one piece of advice I give...*" A little cheesed off with his patronising tone I replied "*Yes, I've been told before - imagine the audience is all naked.*"

He looked startled and replied: "*Well, I was going to say imagine they are all a kindergarten class, but whatever works for you.....*"

James Wills, former editor of the Maldon and Burnham Standard, and now content editor for the Colchester Gazette and a host of weeklies, believes he gives on average at least one talk a week in Essex. Two gems always raise a laugh.

As a young reporter I was on the phone to a senior cabinet minister when the phone suddenly went silent. I declared, using very bad language "*s***, the fat b****d has been cut off.*"

"*No, I am still here*" he replied...

In my first week at the Maldon and Burnham Standard I wrote a blurb about what an honour it was to be Editor. It ended..... *'you may rest assured, under my editorship, the Standard will continue to maintain its reputation for fairness, impartiality and acuracy'*.How can any editor spell accuracy wrong and hope to get away with it?.

Lynne Powell is the editor of Cotswold and Vale magazine and is the former editor of several weekly newspapers in the West and South Midlands. She found she was not a popular speaker when she addressed one organisation on her patch.

As a young editor of a weekly newspaper I was invited to give a talk on making news to a professional women's group. Except they clearly weren't that professional. The speaker booker had muddled her dates 'n' people and the eager audience in front of me were expecting an entertaining evening hearing about 'my' new speed dating business, complete with a have-a-go session with a bunch of game gentlemen. I had wondered why they all looked so glam, and why the room was such a fug of competing sickly perfumes.

As I was there and the dating queen was not, they asked me to go ahead with my talk. No matter how hard I tried, I couldn't make my serious points about journalism engage the bitterly disappointed, now grim-faced lipsticked ladies, who had clearly been hoping for a beguiling bit of romance and couldn't have cared less about making headlines.

Gareth Weekes, former editor of the Salisbury Journal and Bournemouth Echo, found that checking your diary might be a good idea before setting off to give a talk.

As a young editor I was in such a rush that I used to make errors entering appointments in my diary, for example the right day and time but the wrong month. I arrived on the dot of 7.30pm, but exactly a month late, at a village hall to talk to a Women's Institute about the Salisbury Journal. The chairlady told me I should have been there last month. "*Why?*" I replied. "*What happened?*"

Phil Welch, former editor of the Mid Somerset News Series, has always got a good laugh when he has revealed the contents of a genuine For Sale classified advertisement from an American paper. It read: FOR SALE - Tombstone. Grey marble. Unused. Suit someone called Griggs. Tel...

John Butterworth, former editor of the Bromsgrove Advertiser and Shrewsbury Chronicle and now editor of the Black County Bugle, recalls: 'A Shropshire group invited me a year early. I checked with them that it was definitely August 2012 and not 2013 and they said it was. However, when I turned up the place was in darkness. I insisted they paid my petrol for a fruitless journey!'

CHAPTER THREE

THE PRESS GANG

"The Press, Watson, is a most valuable institution, if you only know how to use it."

— *Arthur Conan Doyle, The Adventure of the Six Napoleons / the Adventure of the Crooked Man*

As we have already seen, not every newspaper editor wants to spend time talking to members of the public. Some simply turn down all invitations, while others delegate the task to someone who either has no choice or actually enjoys getting out of the office for a few hours to do something different. For this reason I have devoted a separate chapter to their advice and experiences starting with a former colleague who has some sage advice.

Glyn Monhughes is a senior media lecturer at Liverpool John Moores University and a former regional newspaper reporter, including a spell on the Birmingham Daily News when I was editor.

Standing in front of a diverse group of people and speaking – even for a matter of seconds – is many people's worst nightmare. Others, though, relish the prospect and do so with considerable ease.

So what's the key to success?

There are two keys which will make public speaking easy. Yes, there are other factors which will help create the all-over excellent orator, but the main two things to do when making a speech is to know your subject and to know exactly what it is you are going to say to the audience.

Knowing your subject is vital. What do you do if your notes get lost, or you forget to take them to the event at which you are speaking? What happens if you've put them all onto a USB stick and there's a computer glitch or a power failure? What happens if someone asks you a question and you simply cannot answer.

Once you are certain that you know your subject area, then make sure you know the particular area you are going to tackle. Say you've been asked to talk about the sale of shares in Royal Mail. It's just as well that you know how the stock market works, Government policy towards privatisation, the difficulties that have been encountered over transferring the post carrier to the private sector and so on. That's at the back of your mind. But you need to focus on a few key points.

That's where it is as well to plan what you are going to say. There are various ways of doing this.

You might want to undertake a mind-mapping exercise. Get a blank sheet of paper and put down all the thoughts pertaining to the subject. They don't have to be in any order, but you do need to group similar thoughts together. For example, you may think of the word privatisation. Linked with that might be the following:

Conservative policy tends to favour privatisation.

The Labour Party tends to oppose privatisation.

The 1945-51 Labour Government nationalised the coal and steel industries and brought the railways under state control.

The 1980s privatisations were hugely popular with the public and many people bought shares for the first time.

Privatisation often seen as a dirty word, especially in connection with the NHS.

The Conservative Party has often struggled with the privatisation of Royal Mail.

Once you have the threads of what you want to say, organise these into a talk that flows.

The next thing to take into consideration is how long your speech will be. It it's only five minutes, although you can say a lot in that time, you have to take into consideration the audience's ability to take the facts in. If it's that Royal Mail share sale, you really don't want to be bombarding the listeners with dozens of facts and figures. Think of the headline point you want to make. Remember that, in five minutes, people may remember probably only five points – unless they are writing notes.

Then again, if you are to speak for 45 minutes, you can afford to include many more facts in what it is you will be saying. But spread them out throughout the speech.

Timing is also vitally important. A ten-minute presentation means just that. But remember that you must time your speech by reading it out loud. We read silently at around twice to three times as quickly as when reading a speech out loud.

You must appear calm and confident when you speak in public. As mentioned at the outset of this short piece, you must know your subject matter, and that will aid your confidence. Speaking in an authoritative manner will add to the overall impression you make. You can do this by speaking loudly (but not shouting) and slowly. In one of my other lives – as director of music at a large church in Oxton, Wirral – I frequently come across people who decide that they will read a scripture passage or a poem at a wedding or funeral or will present the eulogy at a funeral. They are unused to public speaking and, often, will be nervous. They are confronted with a sea of faces and they are in a big building. They proceed to read their piece as though reading it out to their nearest and dearest across the breakfast table. It is a rapid mutter and nobody has any idea of what they are saying.

You should always, if you can, rehearse your speech in the venue at which you are speaking. Then you will have some idea of the acoustic and any difficulties you may encounter. Take a friend and ask them to be candid with you about your speaking ability. That same friend should also have been subjected to hearing your speech read out aloud to them – and they should be told to be brutally truthful with you.

Make eye contact with the audience and build in a few dramatic pauses to heighten the impact of what you are saying.

Dress for the part. Make yourself look good. And dress appropriately. Find out about who the audience is and what they might be expecting. Turning up to address a meeting of the CBI dressed in a T-shirt and track suit bottoms might not go down well. And stand comfortably: feet shoulder-width apart gives stability.

Should you use technology? It can be tricky. That said, PowerPoint – though getting a little old-hat – keeps you on track and underlines your key points. But keep it as that. Massively complex slides distract the audience and they'll not be listening to you. You do need to check, though, that your venue will have the equipment to deal with what you need. You may consider using cloud-based storage. Prezi is a very good tool for giving presentations but you do need Internet access to make it work. What happens if there is no Internet available? And what if the system goes down at the last minute? Keep that at the back of your mind.

Some people like to give out handouts. It's a great way to make your point. But giving them out before you speak means that your audience will often be reading the handout, fiddling around with them and making a noise or, even worse, making Origami models. Give them out at the end.

Case Study - In 1994, I was Conservative Parliamentary Candidate for the North Wales European Seat. I made frequent TV appearances and contributed to radio programmes regularly.

One of the major publicity efforts would go into the Conservative Party Conference. At the autumn gathering immediately prior to the election, I was selected to speak in the transport debate. I was keen then, as now, to get more investment in the transport infrastructure in the constituency, so I began to think in headlines.

What could I say which would have maximum impact?

I had four minutes, and that is not very long. And those four minutes gallop by.

So I worked hard on the speech and focused on a few key points. I congratulated the Westminster government on seeing through the project to construct the North Wales expressway, which had helped bring new businesses to the area and had revitalised the Port of Holyhead.

But the railways were lacking, badly. The Cambrian Coast line, from Pwllheli to Machynlleth had received little investment over the years and some stations were closed in the hours of darkness because they had no lighting. So I posed the question: "Are we putting a community's lifeline at risk for the price of a single light bulb?"

That headline brought applause in the hall in Bournemouth, which was heard by those watching the live feed on TV. I was immediately interviewed by the Western Mail and the Daily Post and had prominent coverage the next morning. I also did Welsh and English language interviews for BBC Radio and appeared live on Wales Today for the BBC, Wales Tonight, the HTV news programme and

Newyddion on S4C. There was coverage the next day in the national newspapers.

The result was that I made significant gains in profile through the publicity generated. The speech was taken slowly, made a few strong points and was weighted towards what I thought would be headlines.

Tony Jaffa is a partner in the legal firm Foot Anstey based at Exeter. He and his team are well known to regional newspaper journalists because Tony often has the job of bailing them out (not literally) when they get into legal trouble. He is a regular media conference speaker.

I have not had any professional training in public speaking, so the techniques I use are all based on tips I have picked up over the years. And to my way of thinking, it's simply common sense.

Like everyone else, I imagine, I find public speaking a pretty nerve-wracking experience. But I know for sure that some people are more adept at it than others – though whether that's a skill they have learned or were born with is a moot point.

A few years ago, I was sitting behind a table at a newspaper industry conference as the fourth speaker in a panel of four. The third speaker was an MP, who arrived just a few minutes before the panel discussion began. I couldn't help but notice that as the first and second speakers were on their feet, the MP was busy writing notes literally on the back on an envelope in a small, spiderish, style. When his turn came, he gave an eloquent, amusing, and well-reasoned presentation, as if he had spent hours preparing for this important moment. Of course, I was the only person who knew the truth!

That kind of approach to public speaking takes nerve; you either have it or you don't. That's why I try to adopt a very straightforward approach:

• Spend time on research , to make sure I know more about the subject than the audience;

• speak slowly and breathe normally;

• make sure my notes are written in large font size and the pages are numbered;

• address doors, windows, and (sometimes) specific individuals located on the sides and at the back of the room; and

• most important of all, don't even contemplate trying to tell jokes!

Mistakes can come back to bite you. When I was volunteered to say a few words at my father's 90th birthday, I duly prepared my speech, but forgot to number the pages. So you can guess what happened when I turned two pages over at the same time - I immediately realised there was a problem, but had to ad lib whilst I tried to retrieve the situation. No-one said anything afterwards, so like Basil Fawlty when he attempted not to mention the war to his German guest, I think I got away with that one!

These days, I don't carry out much advocacy. But a few years back, I appeared before magistrates in Bristol to oppose an application by a convicted football hooligan that he should be granted anonymity in any reports of his case. The basis of his application was that although he was an avid supporter of Bristol City, he lived in an area where everyone else supported Bristol Rovers. He claimed that his safety would be in danger if he was exposed as a City fan in the local paper's report of his case. I must say that I was pretty sceptical about this argument, and spent some time challenging him on this issue. Fortunately for me, the magistrates also took the view that this claim was nonsense. In reality, what this hardened thug feared was being teased and ridiculed, not being beaten up.

And then there was the man who applied to the court for an order that a journalist disclose the identity of his source, to assist him in a civil claim he was bringing against a local politician. The applicant was a barrack-room lawyer who had convinced himself that he knew more about the law and court procedure than a mere jumped-up lawyer. Prior to the hearing, he wrote a 178 page letter (not that I managed to read it all!), in which he wrote that it was a shame that we did not live 200 years earlier, because in those days, he would have been able to cut up my client, the journalist, and dispose of him in a lobster pot off the Eddystone Lighthouse. Funnily enough, I managed to raise this 'threat' with the judge at the hearing. I think it's fair to say that His Honour was not amused. His application did not succeed.

But perhaps the most surprising dispute in which I have been involved concerned Smokey and Merlin, cats who live at opposite ends of the country. As a light-hearted attempt to liven up a slow news day, a reporter recorded Smokey's purring on his smartphone, and wrote a piece in which he claimed that Smokey probably had the loudest purr in the world. The owner of Merlin got word of this and complained to the Press Complaints Commission, no less, on the basis that the article was seriously inaccurate because according to the Guinness Book of Records, her Merlin was (and indeed may still be) the cat with the world's loudest purr.

With all due respect to Merlin, I couldn't help feeling that this was hardly the most serious inaccuracy ever to appear in a newspaper. But Merlin's owner doggedly (sorry) purr-sued the complaint (sorry again!), and it was only resolved by the editor agreeing to publish a follow up article about Merlin's purr-fect purring.

Andy Chatfield, Senior Lecturer in Journalism at Southampton Solent University and occasional actor.

Public speaking has become part of my day job now but I have learned a lot from treading the boards as an amateur actor (and one gig as a best man). I think the key thing to remember is that if you are at ease – or at least appear to be – your audience will pay attention. My five tips are:

1. **Target it right.** A joke that has fifty-somethings rolling in the aisles is unlikely to do the trick for 19-year-olds.
2. **Never read out a script.** Rehearse it to time so you know you have enough material, but on the day just use cue cards to keep you on track. You may well find you don't even look at them.
3. **Pace yourself.** I still find myself talking too fast and too much sometimes. Pauses, changes in volume and shifts in tone can have real impact, whether your theme is serious or comical.
4. **Look at the audience**. Eye contact with one person can magically engage a roomful. If you are brave enough to make it a little interactive by asking questions, even better.
5. **Dare to ask for feedback.** If you intend to become a regular speaker, the best judges are your last audience. Ask those you trust for constructive but honest criticism.

I do recall a number of farewell speeches in newsrooms when the departing editor/sub/reporter decided unwisely to use the platform to settle a few scores - often with the senior managers they were too meek to confront one-to-one during their long career. It never works in my opinion, but it might have made them feel better.

Former Radio Devon presenter and local newspaper reporter Lincoln Shaw has entertained many audiences over the years, although, he tells me, he prefers to play golf nowadays.

Way, way back in the mists of time, when I was the most junior reporter on the Berwick Journal I went to a Labour-ish meeting to report a talk by an eminent visiting speaker about Keir Hardie. Chatting up the great man in advance I confessed I had never heard of Keir Hardie. Upon which he began his talk by pointing to me, recalling our conversation and shaking his head at the ignorance of youth. It taught me a valuable lesson. Disguise your ignorance.

Another embarrassing experience was when I was despatched to the annual dinner of the very posh Berwick Motoring Club and arrived in a rather faded brown suit--my only one in those hard up times-- and brown boots--to find everyone else resplendent in evening dress. They were all snobs but very kind.

I had a further embarrassing moment when I was still young and callow. I arrived at a dinner given for the Press by the brand new Development Corporation set up to create the New Town of Corby, the Northamptonshire steel town (sadly no longer). Hospitality was lavish and we were all invited to help ourselves and pour ourselves top quality brandy into huge glasses. It was an experience new to me so I filled it nearly to the brim. The chairman, a titled gent, in his speech promised that they would build a fine new town adding, with a glance in my direction: "*If we have any money left when Mr Shaw has finished his brandy*". But at least it made him remember me. Some time later he offered me the job of press officer to the Corporation which, thank God, I declined.

Roll on a century or so later and I gave a talk to a church group at Babbacombe, all of whom had enjoyed a splendid lunch. I obviously wasn't doing very well. I saw one or two eyelids drooping and, in the front row, an old lady in a wheelchair not only fell fast asleep but was snoring loudly. I cast a worried glance at the chairwoman who was quite re-assuring and said: *"Don't worry Mr Shaw she always does that and can hear every word you are saying"*. Adding fiercely: *"Wake up Mabel"*.

There have been many other embarrassments including finding that a Brixham lunch club had double booked myself and another speaker due to talk about local history. Which one would lose the toss and leave ? Neither, in the end, because we found a common theme and did a splendid double act that was rated as one of the best talks they had ever had.

One busy week when I was working full time for BBC Radio Devon I was asked to give a talk to an organisation with a county-wide membership in a hall in Dawlish which, when I arrived, was packed with people replete after lunch and drinks. It had been a busy day and while I was sitting in a chair trying to collect my thoughts I heard two women at a table nearby discussing the speaker

"Who is he ?'

"Dunno, never heard of him, bet it will be very dull. Let's sit near the back and if he's no good we can slip out".

Indignation steeled my nerves and I began my talk by recalling this conversation without, of course identifying the two concerned. I said: *"Ladies I have my eyes on you and if you move towards the door I shall abandon this talk and be out before you"* It raised a laugh and a couple of red faces that stayed put and applauded (no doubt hypocritically) when I had finished my spiel.

Katie Jarvis, who writes for Cotswold Life, is in great demand as a speaker. Here she recounts some of her more hilarious moments.

A friend of mine – a local radio presenter – often gives talks to WIs. To mitigate boredom and to add an aura of intimacy, he'll often write down names mentioned during the 'business' session, before he speaks, which he'll interweave in a humorous way into his talk. One particular WI was very insistent that the business session was private and made him wait outside while they conducted it. At a slight loss, he put his ear to the door and wrote down any names he could make out.

As usual, he began his talk by jocularly including these names as he went along – only to be greeted by horrified silence. What he'd failed to make out was that these were the names of members who had recently died.

In my own talk, I often include the following incidents, which are personal to me.

When I worked on the Stroud News and Journal, our wonderful old-school editor, Dennis Mason, insisted on traditional values. This was particularly the case when it came to writing up the frequent wedding reports with which we were presented. Every time a new member of staff joined, Dennis would give the usual lecture: "*There are no grooms in my paper's weddings. Only bridegrooms.*" One day, a new recruit listened to this instruction with due care, and diligently typed out a wedding report, which appeared the next week. It read, "*The bride, who used to work as a bridegroom...*" Dennis had failed to take account of the equestrian nature of the Stroud area.

When I was a sub editor, one particular reporter – Jonathan - who worked in a district office, was fantastic at providing crime stories – mainly (I'm convinced) as he was personally involved in them; but hopeless when it came to accuracy. He drove me absolutely mad. One day, he filed a story about a man named 'Oneill', without an apostrophe.

Our conversation, by telephone, went as follows:

Me: *'Jonathan, O'Neill has an apostrophe'.*

Jonathan (realising I'm very cross and slightly worried): *'Honestly, Katie, it doesn't.'*

Me (now incandescent): *'Jonathan, I've NEVER heard of O'Neill without one. Check!'*

Jonathan: *'I already have. Truly.'*

Me: *'WELL CHECK AGAIN!'*

Long pause. Phone rings. Jonathan (absolutely sincerely): *'I've checked and it doesn't have an apostrophe... But he's decided he'd like to start using one.'*

At the Stroud News and Journal, we cub reporters wanted the fires, the murders, the armed robberies. What we got were the golden weddings. And what we had to ask was, *"Where did you meet?"* and *"What is the secret of your long marriage?"* The answer to the second was always the same. My friend and fellow reporter Sandra went to the top of Stroud to interview one 50th anniversary couple, who gave the usual answers. *"What was the secret of their long marriage?"* *"Give and take,"* they replied. *"And never going to bed on an argument."* After a few minutes, the chap disappeared off to make a cup of tea. As he left, the wife leaned towards Sandra and said, *"Actually, he's a miserable old bugger, and I want you to print that."*

Katie's news editor at the Stroud News and Journal was Sandra Ashenford.

I have talked to many audiences over the years, young and old, but more in the form of teaching/ lecturing rather than public speaking. In my early years in journalism I also taught at the local further education college on their media course each week. I did the print journalism bit, which nobody really wanted to learn, because they all wanted to be radio presenters or film directors.

I had a lot of trouble getting them to turn up or do any assignments. In the end, the course leader got really heavy with them and pointed out they would fail the whole course if they didn't pass the print journalism module. After that they turned up - but two of them would then just settle down and sleep through the two-hour session. I left them to it because at least they weren't causing any problems!

Now, as well as teaching children at a local museum, I go out and give lots of talks to care homes and groups such as Rotary, taking with me various "mystery objects" from our handling collection. These sessions are full of humour as people try to work out what the objects are.

Andrew Howard spent his early years as a journalist on the Craven Herald based in Skipton and the Dales. For many years he was deputy editor of the Express and Echo in Exeter before setting up his own company in 2013. He recalls the trouble of forgetting the age gap when speaking to school children.

Having been a reporter in Skipton I moved to the Express & Echo in Exeter where I worked for almost 20 years. I was asked to give a talk to a class of 12- to 13-year-olds in an Exeter secondary school on working in newspapers, and afterwards asked if there were any questions. As well as the usual 'how *much do you earn'* (I think I handled this well by saying 'not as much as teacher'), I was asked if I knew any famous people.

Recalling my beat in the Dales I reeled off a list: Fred Trueman, Don Mosey, Michael Parkinson, Richard Whiteley, Russell Harty...

...they'd not heard of a single one of them, which put me back in my box.

Then there was the time at a colleague's leaving do when he had, for his last job, had to cover an interminable week-long public inquiry into yet another planned bypass*"Bypass, bypass, bypass,"* he muttered into his pint. *"If I ever hear the word bypass again I swear I'll scream."*

To which the bloke behind us angrily replied: "What's *wrong with you? My dad's just had a bypass operation and it saved his life!"*

My favourite joke I told many an audience goes back to when I was working on the Craven Herald in Skipton and the days when it had nothing but adverts on the front page, typeset in glorious hot metal Monotype. One week, the largest, boldest one was from a pet charity: *Wanted, good homes for cats, dogs, and rabbis.*

Even modern computer spellcheckers would let that one go by, mind you.

Then there was the "25 years ago" column, a pretty dull job given to trainees as a way of

 a: teaching them about the history of the area and the paper and

b: filling space!

I did one which briefly referenced a report on the record top price of a ram for sale at the local auction mart a quarter of a century previously. Skipton, as the name suggests, was a town where sheep played an important economic role, after all.

On the day of publication, into the office came a red-faced son of the soil saying: *"Can't you people remember anything? I told you 25 years ago it was a tup, not a ram!"*

Priceless! And a lesson in how some readers never forget.

Daniel Wainwright, political editor of the Shropshire Star, found his audience quizzed him on national not local events.

I went to give a talk to the Wolverhampton branch of the National Pensioners' Convention. After being greeted with stony-faced silence I subjected myself to a question and answer session expecting it to be about my views on the media, politics, councils etc.

Instead I was asked whether or not I would arm the rebels in Syria and what I personally planned to do about ending secret courts of protection.

I sort of had to imagine myself as in the same boat as Liverpool footballer Steven Gerrard would be if, fresh from a humiliating defeat, he suddenly found himself asked not about his team's tactics but on whether or not Britain should go ahead with HS2 rail scheme.

There was another occasion where I went to report on the speech given by another person – the West Midlands MEP Mike Nattrass. He had recently resigned from UKIP and his speech to the pensioners was to be his first public engagement on our patch since leaving.

We waited and waited and there was no sign of him. The pensioners were adamant that he'd said he was coming. This, they said, was backed up by the fact that *it's been in the paper'*.

Yes, it had been in the paper. It had been in the paper because I'd put it there.

I'd put it there because they had sent me a press release to tell people he was coming.

In the end it turned out that he'd actually cancelled on them some weeks ago and there had been 'cross purposes'.

Former television journalist and investigate reporter John Kiddey remembers being stumped by one member of the audience in the usual question and answer session after the main talk.

As a reporter on the local BBC TV News "Look East" I was often asked to give talks to groups such as the Women's' Institutes. One dark winter's night in deepest fenland Cambridgeshire I addressed a gathering of the WI and, being a progressive chap, I thought they would appreciate a talk about "what IS news"?

I spent half an hour explaining how news is gathered, who decides what news is, how news is influenced by political, social and other interest groups. In Thatcherite Britain of 1984, it seemed to me to be a topic laden with promise for heated discussion.

When I had finished, the chairwoman stepped forward and asked *"Does anyone have any questions for Mr Kiddey?"* Instantly a lady put her hand up and said ....

"Is that a wig your newsreader wears or is it her hair real?" I was speechless .....

Owen Jones formerly of the North Devon Journal and now with Devon Life recalls how a flattering invitation turned into a disaster.

I count myself in that group that doesn't enjoy the experience of public speaking. I recall once being asked by a rather attractive teacher to speak to some of the girls at her school. Flattered, I agreed on the understanding that it was to be an informal chat about working in newspapers with perhaps half a dozen sixth form students over coffee. But when I arrived I was told the event had been oversubscribed so half the school was seated in a huge hall waiting to be entertained. I was totally thrown, gave an awful speech and was rewarded with a smattering of polite applause. A few weeks later I ran into one of the sixth formers in a local pub, where she loudly declared it had been the most boring speech they had ever heard. I think that put me off for life.

Sometimes a few well chosen words can have the maximum impact on an audience as Donna MacAllister, now a reporter on the Inverness Courier discovered. She believed part of her most amusing speech would never be printed, but she was wrong. She recalls:

It was my leaving do after working at the Cornishman. I was a very serious minded young journalist at the time, and probably not the easiest person to work with as getting the story meant everything to me – and I mean 'everything'. I trampled on toes, we could say. So, anyway, just as the glasses were clinking I looked at my colleagues all sitting around me and I started my farewell speech with the sentence: " I am sorry for being a bitch."

CHAPTER FOUR

VIEWS FROM

THE PEWS

Don't give up, Moses was a basketcase too – sign outside an American church

Some of the best (and worst) speeches I have heard have come on a Sunday morning. They are called sermons. In recent times they have also provided me with a host of good jokes to tell when I have been lecturing young journalists.

I am reliably informed by the Rev Andrew Green, who writes in this section, that his sermons can take at least 12 hours of solid preparation. I am pleased to say that his hard work has paid off as far as I am concerned.

I was distinctly unimpressed with the sermons I heard when in my teens and things didn't improve until I moved to Torquay in 1990. Since then I have made up for lost time, something I am extremely grateful for.

The Rev David Coffey is a former President of the Baptist World Alliance and one of the most sought after speakers in the UK and abroad.

A minister was the guest preacher at a village church for their harvest thanksgiving services. The tradition in this village church was to provide lunch for the preacher after the morning service and it was served in a room where the preacher ate alone. Straight after lunch the preacher would be returning to preach at the afternoon service.

The church served the preacher his lunch. This was the largest plate of sausages and mash he had ever seen. Knowing he had to stay awake to preach at the afternoon service, the preacher decided he was unable to eat this huge meal, so he took three of the sausages and wrapped them in his handkerchief and put them his pocket.

During his afternoon sermon, he felt a sneeze coming on and without thinking- he pulled out his handkerchief, and to the bemusement of the congregation, three sausages rolled down the aisle!

I was lecturing in Zaire(now Democratic Republic of Congo) to a diverse multi-lingual audience and had to give my talk through three interpreters. In my opening comments, I said I had been on the road for three weeks and was missing my family at home in the UK, especially my beautiful wife Janet. The English linguists told me afterwards, the phrase 'beautiful wife' translated well into French and Swahili. But the Lingala interpreter gave a completely different meaning to my phrase when he said - *'David says he is missing his big fat mama!'*

A professor of theology from Oxford was visiting a remote village in Southern Africa. He was invited to preach at the village church on the Sunday morning and thought he would take a sermon that had gone down well with his university students. He was totally dependent on his interpreter when he stood up to preach his sermon. He began his message to the rural congregation by saying: *'I want to look at a verse from John's Gospel which attempts to address the big existential questions that highlight the ground of our being and the nature of the eternal God and his relationship to the cosmos.'* The interpreter gulped and said to the congregation: *'The preacher says he is very happy to be with us in church this morning'.*

A British academic was giving a university lecture in China. Prior to the lecture he was introduced to his interpreter and asked him whether it would be helpful to go over the substance of his address. The interpreter said this would not be necessary. He began his lecture and after a few sentences he paused so the interpreter could provide a translation. The interpreter indicated for him to say a little more. After a few sentences he paused and the interpreter said to the audience in Mandarin: *'I have heard enough to tell you that this lecturer will not say anything you have not heard before'*

The lecturer continued and was amazed when the interpreter repeatedly indicated to the lecturer to keep speaking. The lecturer thought this was just an amazing feat of memory and that the interpreter had chosen to summarise his lecture at key stages in order to maintain the flow of the lecture.

When the speaker did occasionally pause, the interpreter would say to the audience: *'I am convinced this man has nothing new to say to us'* or *'you could have spent your time better'* or *'no, he has said nothing new yet'*

The lecture proceeded in this fashion until the speaker came to conclusion and when he sat down, the interpreter said to the audience: *'As I anticipated, this lecturer did not have one new idea to share- but please applaud anyway to show your appreciation'*!

The Rev Ted Holmes was Associate Pastor and Administrator at Forest Hills Baptist Church in Nashville, Tennessee. In 2008 he began working for the International Mission Board (IMB) of the Southern Baptist Convention, USA. Currently, he is an IMB Team Strategy Leader in Warsaw, Poland.

Wedding ceremonies and what is said bring to mind some funny stories, especially those that are officiated by a father who happens to also be the minister.

At my oldest daughter Jennifer's wedding I was waxing eloquently when a fly landed upon the bride's nose. Now with her back turned to the congregation, the only people who could see this was myself and my other daughter, Lindsay, who was the maid of honour. The fly immediately flew away after a quick twitch of the nose, but the damage had already been done. My daughters' eyes met and they began giggling as the congregation smiled and wondered if they had missed a joke. I, on the other hand, was sending very stern glances to them both, trying not to lose my composure. A little silent discipline was all that was needed as they both pulled it together. Not wanting another potentially embarrassing moment, our second daughter Lindsay, wisely chose someone other than her father to officiate at her wedding.

Just a month or two before Jennifer's wedding, I attended another wedding, in which a friend of mine, Wayne, our Minister of Music, was officiating at his daughter's nuptials. My friend is well-known for having a great sense of humour and for always knowing what to say at the right time. He has a very quick wit similar to that of Robin Williams. Beverly and I noticed at the beginning of the service that Wayne was behaving himself very well. His daughter had laid down the law. No jokes. She wanted a dignified wedding, one which would be consecrated to the Lord, and would be an appropriate celebration of beginning a new life together with her groom.

Wayne conducted the service in a wonderful fashion, and the bride was very proud of her father ... until the very end. We were all anxiously awaiting the moment when he would say, "*I now pronounce you to be husband and wife, and you may now kiss the bride.*" But, as only a father could do, he finished the phrase with "*... And you may now hold hands.*" The groom kissed her anyway, but maybe not as long as he wished.

A friend who lives in the southern state of Georgia in the US is Alan Morris, the Area Missionary for the North Central Baptist Associations of Georgia. He said that one Sunday he was scheduled to preach at a small church in North Georgia. Just before the service was to begin a rather large and tall young man dressed in camouflage sat down on the front pew. My friend Alan went over to introduce himself and wanting to strike up a conversation, jokingly said to him, "*I didn't see you there,*" – referring to his camouflage.

The young man replied in a North Georgia slow drawl, as serious as he could be, "*Well, I'm big enough. Can't see how you didn't see me.*"

And then he asked Alan: "*I bet chya' can't guess where I'm goin' after the service today?*"

Playing along Alan said: "*No, where ya' going?*"

"*I'm goin' hunt'n.*"

"*Really,*" Alan said, "*I never would have guessed. Are you an avid hunter?*"

"*Naw, deer, '* came the man's reply.

One of my favorite jokes I like to tell when giving a talk is about a Texas rancher who marries a mail-order bride. The old rancher had just loaded his new bride into the wagon and was headed home at a good clip when the horse stopped and refused to pull the wagon.

The rancher got out of the wagon, faced the horse and said, "*That's one!*"

With a, Giddiup! they continued on for a while and the horse stopped again. Again he got out of the wagon and said to the horse, "*That's two!*"

Again they went for a good distance when the horse began prancing and jerking its head around not a bit happy having to pull the wagon.

This time the old rancher stopped the wagon and grabbed a long piece of wood from the back of the wagon , went and stood before the horse and said "*That's three!*" Then he hauled off and smacked the horse right along side the head as hard as he could.

The horse staggered and almost dropped to its knees, then straightened giving full attention, as they got under way, to the serious job of pulling the wagon. The bride who was shocked at what the rancher had done spoke sharply to her new husband, "*I don't think you should have hit that poor horse the way you did.*" The old rancher didn't even look at her but spoke loud and clear, "*That's one!*"

The Rev Andrew Green is senior pastor at Upton Vale Baptist Church who has preached throughout the United Kingdom and abroad.

Preaching has been one of the most important parts of my ministry and consequently I have given it significant time. I have found that having one day each week set aside exclusively for preparation has been a great help. I can deal with the crises and dramas of ministry on the other six days, as long as I know I have that one day "protected" for preparation. My notes are carefully prepared – so my worst nightmare would be to lose my notes just before I came to preach!

Over the years I have had to cope with all sorts of distractions while preaching. Several times people have fainted or been unwell during a service, often there has been a continually crying child. Once, when I was preaching at an evening service, a young girl with adenoid problems started snoring loudly. I was actually "preaching with a view" at this Surrey church and was eventually invited to come as their minister. I have since wondered whether a boxed set of my sermons might be marketed to people with sleep problems!

Preaching through an interpreter is a challenge and the phrase "lost in translation" has been apt for my attempts at speaking in another culture and language. In both Bangladesh and Thailand I was translated sentence by sentence and realized (too late) that so much of my language is metaphor and idiom – which simply does not work! I looked out at a congregation totally mystified with regard to what I was going on about!

When I was younger I regularly did Children's Addresses and they sometimes went spectacularly wrong, One Easter I spoke on 1 Corinthians 15 explaining that more than 500 people had seen the Resurrected Jesus at one time. My point was that normally we don't see dead men coming to life and would not believe the witness of one person on their own – but we are more likely to believe the truth of an extraordinary event if it was witnessed by hundreds of people. Since that Easter we had a congregation of about 500, I did something "extraordinary": I ate a daffodil. I nearly gagged at that moment, and when I preached the sermon I noticed that I was constantly exhaling bits of daffodil that had stuck to my wind pipe!

Weddings are always a delight, but again proper preparation is essential. I find that the bride and groom almost always have an embarrassing middle name and need to get over their giggles before the actual day. I also like the bride to practice walking up the church isle and up the steps to the platform. On one memorable occasion the bride stepped on her dress as she ascended the steps. Suddenly all the buttons at the back of her dress popped. With commendable practicality the mother of the bride simply stepped up with safety pins and the organist kept on playing! Many brides would have dissolved in tears, but this lovely lady saw the humour of the situation and laughed and laughed. It made the day!

Graham McBain is Associate Pastor and head of Adult Ministries at Upton Vale.

A few years ago while planning a visit to a church in the South of England I was told: *'You'll meet our prophet'*.

I was very excited – what does a prophet look like? Flowing robes and a long beard?

He actually turned out to be a fairly normal chap – worked in the accounts department at the local council. He said he heard God speak to him *' become a prophet'* so he took to dressing in a multi coloured striped tunic and carrying a big thick wooden rain stick around with him which he would bang on the floor whilst *' prophesying'*.

It was a very, very strange experience preaching in a fairly elderly church with this colourful character in the front row who then after the service stepped up on stage, took the microphone and told me and the church the prophecy plus the word from God he had for me.

With his head was bowed, his robes swishing and his stick banging he prophesied - all recorded on cassette.

The question for me: was it a word from God or not?

I don't want to mock the man. I believe he was sincere. And his prophecy was very picturesque: I was an archeologist uncovering a fine, precious set of clothes.

But he went on to say (in my current context) I would be a spiritual Father to many people.

Did the prophecy come true? I don't know.

Was it from God? Maybe.

Did it encourage me? Definitely.

Did I hear from God?

The Rev Mark Searle is the Priest in Charge at St Mary Magdalene Church in Torquay town centre. It was only after he started public speaking and at theological college that he discovered he was dyslexic which meant he had to change the entire way he gave sermons and talks.

I trained as an actor and attended two top drama schools, but finding work was not easy. I had a part in one episode of Grange Hill, did the occasional television advert and had some parts in plays but it wasn't any sort of living. Ironically I could earn more per hour than my doctor father did working at Exeter Hospital, but that was no good when I only worked three days a year!

The first time I made any sort of speech was at my wedding and it terrified me. It was the standard thank yous to everyone involved, but beforehand I was told there were so many unspoken rules about what to say and who to thank that come the day I was scared I would miss someone out. I had a small notebook in which I wrote one line per page to remind me of everything I wanted to say, but it was an experience I did not enjoy.

Soon after I was invited to speak to a large church youth group on the subject of 'God, sex and rock n' roll'. I sweated over what I would say and eventually decided to use my father's template. He is a good speaker and so I copied his style of writing everything down word for word. It was dreadful and made me realize that if I was to address an audience again I would do it in my style and not anybody else's.

Two months later I gave a different talk to the entire congregation one Sunday morning and this time I adopted the totally different approach of putting three images on a screen and speaking off the cuff about them. I felt truly at home doing it that way and realized this was the best way for me in future. It was also the first time I really felt God's calling. Of course I had no idea what lay ahead.

When I eventually gave up on any hopes of fame as an actor I went to theological college but continued to struggle when it came to public speaking. They gave me lots of training, but it didn't suit me. Then I discovered why I wasn't making any progress – I am dyslexic. It wasn't until I met up with an educational psychologist that I was given the tools to get what was in my head out in such a way that other people would understand. I was introduced to the concept of mind mapping which is ideal for someone who is a visual rather than linear thinker. I have used mind mapping ever since. I have one supreme thought and I build and shape my sermons round it. I have found that this gives me the opportunity to look at my audience, see how they are reacting and detect their mood.

I like to think I have not dropped too many clangers, but you can never plan for the unexpected. At my previous church in Ashtead, Surrey, I had a challenging message for the evening service's congregation in which I outlined the church's history and then moved on to what I thought was next. About a third of the way through I was interrupted by a man who said: "I think you are criticising all of us here". It led to a 50 minute open discussion where they let rip about my leadership style and where they felt I was going wrong. My wife still refers to it as 'Black Sunday'. It ended well and helped clear the air by giving some people the chance to have their say about problems that had been building up long before I was involved. That didn't make it any less painful at the time, but we moved on together afterwards.

I guess most speakers have had moments when what has come out of their mouths has been different from what they really wanted to say. I read out the banns for one couple and called them Sarah and Rachel when it should have been Sarah and Richard. He quickly stood up and corrected me. On another occasion I said Sted and Ella rather than Ed and Stella.

My most eye-catching moment came when the bride and groom at one wedding knelt in front of me to pray and someone stood on the back of her dress, opening up her entire front. I am glad I reacted quickly and gave her my book to cover her front.

CHAPTER FIVE

TALK OF

THE TOWN

"A newspaper is more interesting when somebody across the table is reading it" — Irak Ibrahim Hussain Didi

Marcus Wood was a Conservative candidate at both the 2005 and 2010 General Elections. He found himself in hot water when he was too honest at one meeting.

Political speeches are always a nightmare...especially when (as is often the case) the hosting organisation is 'non-political' and asks you to make a non-partisan speech. Many will remember Tony Blair being slow hand-clapped by the women's Institute audience in 2000...well, very soon after being selected to be a Parliamentary candidate in 2002 I knew exactly how he felt.

First things first; as the glowing new prospective MP for a prosperous southern seaside town, I made the huge mistake of believing that people really did want to know my views of things, and really did want politicians to speak their minds.

Just how wrong can you be?

One of the very earliest 'gigs' I did was in a neighbouring constituency; the MP there was from my party and at the very last minute became unable to attend a local event. My agent, in his wisdom, thought it a great opportunity for me to raise my profile and offered me as an alternative speaker. As a consequence, and with less than an hour's notice, I found myself on a December evening in a slightly damp and cold Victorian village hall sitting on the stage at a small wooden table alongside the meeting chairman and some secretary or other facing a far larger than expected audience of about 70 people.

Now several 'political public speaking' rules had already been broken, the most important of which was that I didn't have time to find out much about who these people were or, more importantly, why they had gathered to hear me speak.

The meeting started very well, the mostly elderly folk were obviously happy that I had made the journey (far out into a very dark Devon valley) and applauded loudly when I was introduced and all seemed well. I bumbled through as best I could, trying to avoid anything confrontational, party political or controversial. I waffled about integrity and the need for greater public involvement in politics and explained why I had come into politics, background on the family, usual stuff, and then – as I prefer to do in these events – cut to a questions and answer session.

Political speakers fall into groups. Most (including Margaret Thatcher, Michael Howard and Winston Churchill) are assiduous script readers. They will draft and write every word of their speeches and ensure they deliver them as written – often after several rehearsals. These politicians often have a lawyer's training and know that a misplaced word, however minor, can change the meaning or perception of a phrase and therefore each and every word must be spoken exactly as scripted. Others (such as David Cameron, Tony Blair and Ken Clarke) are better at improvising and prefer to read using simple prompt cards with bullet point notes of the main points they wish to make, adlibbing the exact phrasing on the day. These politicians are more susceptible to attack but they come across in the media as more 'human'.

There is a very small third group – into which I would put myself – who make no preparations whatsoever, shoot entirely from the hip and, as a result, do a great job of appearing 'normal' but get themselves and their political parties into terrible and often irretrievable disasters every time they speak in public.

Wisely, politicians from the first two groups try their hardest to avoid public question and answer sessions whereas I regularly used to do them, figuring that the audience usually loved the interaction.

Sure enough, the session went well to begin with; Europe was batted off to the future with ease, questions about our (then) wobbly party leader were avoided (I thought) rather elegantly. Question three was from a rather red-faced man in his sixties – clearly a minor bigwig judging by the reaction to his question from the rest of the audience.

"Mr. Wood, what are your views on spending more public money on railways?" Unbeknown to him, I had just spent 15 of the previous 48 hours on various delayed, diverted and dirty trains during a disastrous business trip to Manchester, pondering the exact same question.

So without thinking I offered my opinion. "In my work I have to travel a fair bit, in fact I drive about 20,000 miles annual on business – mostly conducting interviews for clients as part of my work as a head-hunter for industry. Every so often I try and use the trains instead, partly because I keep getting bouts of green conscience and partly because people keep telling me I am 'mad' to drive all the time and that the train is less stressful.

"And every time I do, I am left with the same feelings of puzzlement. How could anyone think that a trip on Britain's railways isn't more stressful than driving – or flying, even? On the trip I have just made, train times, platforms and routes were changed at will, with no warning and often no announcements. My return train was delayed, then cancelled without apology or alternative being offered, so my trip stretched from five hours (already an hour longer than driving) to seven and a half hours.

"The entire infrastructure is ancient and out of date. The best any government has managed to do at a cost of billions is slap paint over a few stations and smarten up the trains – it's like putting lipstick on a pig."

I mistook the hushed silence. Thinking the audience were breathlessly awaiting my prescription to right this ill, I ploughed on: "This trip yet again refreshed my long held view that the railways are an outmoded, inefficient, inflexible and pointless form of public transport."

My agent was gesticulating something from the back of the hall but I had warmed to my theme now and wasn't going to be distracted. "We happily dumped the canals when a cheaper and more efficient form of transport arrived, so why did we maintain the railways when they were in turn superseded by the automobile and the plane?

"Why do we insist on maintaining thousands and thousands of miles of ancient, crumbling Victorian infrastructure – the platforms and the rails dictate that in the 21st century we are still using heavy, steel-wheeled train sets that are inefficient, expensive to run and terribly inflexible? Steel works and ancient track signalling means massive gaps between trains for safety so while a motorway is utilised all the time, a rail line spends most of its life empty, all that precious land wasted for 90% of the time. Most of the train sets operating today were built in the 1970s – just think how far the car has evolved since then; how much more efficient and economical they are. Our trains are Austin allegro's in a Toyota Prius age.)

I was really pleased with this catchy (headline grabbing?) sound bite, and eagerly I launched the finale to my blinding vision of the future.

"The much maligned Dr. Beeching was quite right, but he didn't go anything like far enough. Wouldn't it have made sense years ago to rip up all the tracks and points and instead lay tarmac roadways long the routes and put large bendy-bus-style road coaches on there than can overtake each other, turn round, stop quickly and where you could introduce real competition and flexibility?

"Yes, we need public transport, perhaps more than ever before. But unless we are prepared to allow the public transport system to evolve properly we are doomed. Instead of letting the train take the strain, we will continue to drive and let the earth take the strain instead. And that would be much worse in the long run."

You could have heard a pin drop and even I couldn't help notice that my agent appeared to have fainted. The red-faced man got rather slowly to his feet and said in a slow and slightly menacing tone "Do I understand you correctly? You would rip up thousands of miles of our railway network, scrap all our trains entirely and replace them with buses."

For the first time my confidence took a wobble. Whether it was the soft hissing from several members of the gathering when I mentioned "*Dr Beeching*" or the gasps from many others when I said '*bendy bus*' but the horrible reality was beginning to dawn on me that my up to now hospitable and polite 'non political' audience might be a little less docile than I had imagined.

"Is this your party's policy?" shouted a man from the back, his rising voice both incredulous and indignant. "What about the workers?" called another. There were several mutterings from members present, and not in my support. I overheard comments like "outrageous", "typical bloody politicians", "Well I won't be voting

93

for them' and "utter madness.." "well look what they did to the miners..."

Too late my eyes were drawn to the village notice board at the back of the hall. I could make out "Village Preservation Society"...and then my eyes made out more words ".... Steam Railway"....."Meeting here"....."Meet the MP.... All welcome" "Come and join the fight to protect our heritage".

It was too late, my urgent protestations that the views expressed where my own and nothing to do with my party fell on deaf ears. I spouted about published party manifesto plans to build newer, cleaner and faster trains but it was no use. By now the once pleasant English country folk gathered respectfully to hear a prospective Parliamentarian speak were now an openly scornful and hostile baying pack.

Realising there was a danger of the first case of public disorder in his village for 300 years, the chairman of the meeting put me out of my misery by declaring the meeting over, 40 minutes ahead of schedule.

It turned out that about half the audience were shareholders and members of the local steam railway company. God alone knows how many votes I lost for my MP colleague that night but I was more relieved that he was when he was re-elected the following year.

Ian Handford JP has introduced hundreds of speakers and is a much-in-demand speaker in his own right. He is a local historian who has done much to revive interest in Torbay's chequered history.

Over the past 30 plus years I guess I have done literally thousands of public presentations sometimes in a political vane, sometimes as a magistrate and most recently - the last 13 years - in my capacity as chairman of Torbay Civic Society which opens up environmental, conservation and preservation, but most importantly of all, historically based stories of either a person's biography or about our heritage.

This has brought about or involved a number of funny or quirky incidents.

It came as a surprise to discover the speaker finder at one gathering out in 'the sticks' had managed to double book me and another speaker on the same day on the same subject. On arrival neither of us particularly wanted to walk away having done our research on Castle Drogo. We decided to toss a coin in front of the audience – that was a first – and I lost, so that day for all my trouble I was rewarded with a cup of tea.

Magistrates are often confronted with very strange situations in court. I well recall one December 24th when in the chair to have a homeless yet drunken women in the dock who had already spent most of the night in a cell. We always have to ask defendants *"have you got anything to say in your defence"* to which she very quickly replied *"well it is Christmas Eve"* which I thought was brilliant and dismissed the case as time served.

Years ago Michael Heseltine, when Minister at the Department of Trade and Industy, was in front of a large audience of businessmen explaining how his department had made decisions responding to a deregulation issue by getting rid of a number of outdated regulations from the statute book. When pressed to confirm just one he picked the "Weed Act", a law introduced in the mid 1930s - now gone. I then rather unwisely asked: *"Can you tell us how many farmers were prosecuted under the Act, Minister"*. On turning to his civil servant the answer was – one. One in over half a century was hardly what the business community had been looking for when turning for help!

Then there is the issue of you the speaker being caught out, and this usually occurs in questions after your presentation. This famous person's children? What happened to them? Well, in the case of Flora Thompson or Charles Babbage or Nelson's child by Florence let alone Lady Hamilton and many other individuals, I had no idea. One trick to get out of the problem is to state one you do know like Brunel; his son Henry went on to be almost as famous as his father yet has always been overlooked due to having such a famous father. The best answer though is to just be honest, no historian can possibly follow through a whole family on descendents unless they just specialise on one name – my list covers well over 200.

Presenting to children is always dangerous fun; they have a knack of catching out even the most experienced of us. I well recall playing Father Christmas to a party of children at a Pontins Camp at Paignton during the 1970's only to be caught out when one bright spark shouted out, look at those Wellingtons, he's that bloke with the big feet – get out of that when you take a size 12.

On the other hand when a mixed audience of children and adults were once asked to create the longest sentence they could devise while still making sense one bright spark soon came up with an answer – life Imprisonment.

I love the story of a politician who when handed his notes by his civil servant then delivered his speech without checking it first. He immediately got a resounding response from his audience before utter silence set in as he read it out exactly the same a second time; his civil servant had forgotten to keep the carbon copy himself and had left the two sets pinned together, so the Minister read out both sets – one after the other.

Having motored to a venue at Exeter I discovered the speaker finder had written in Charles Dickens (parents had a home at Exeter) as the subject for the talk, whereas he had actually asked me to tell the story of Admiral Fitzroy – the famous captain who had taken Darwin around the world. Fitzroy was a strong Christian who later committed suicide when his Origin of Species hit the bookstalls. Almost lost for words, I pointed out that Fitzroy eventually set up the Met Office and proved the value of the barometer to all at sea, so I got back to an Exeter link where the Met Office is today.

At one speaking engagement I noticed a presenter had his fly open, something I now always check before stepping forth onto any stage. One boring speaker, who really was going on too long, also had the same problem and I watched as a piece of paper went around his audience until about 40 people later he was passed it to read – your fly is open. He immediately sat down which ended the presentation.

I was once confronted with a chairman who liked the sound of his own voice and while introducing me as the speaker on the newly introduced Uniform Business Rates and how they would enjoy the detail, went on to cover how the new system would work, who it would cover, how the new phasing and transitional relief would affect all those who paid business rates. It was indeed a quite brilliant précis of the subject I had travelled more than 80 miles to do. He finally, turned to me and said: " *I give you our specialist spokesman Ian Handford"* and sat down. I stood up and said: *'Any questions?'* and got an amazing response.

Questioning techniques are interesting. I was once asked why should I be given the job rather than all the others being interviewed at a rather long day of interviews for a job in Exeter. I gave what I thought were all the usual sensible answers- I have a good past record of experience, would be loyal, and was honest and was available and did not have to give a long notice period. I didn't get the job, but it was a good question I often used myself when I became an employer of others.

When speaking to anyone always be aware of where you are in a room. On one occasion I was one of a party of four allowed into a government minister's meeting in London. We marched in, sat down, said what we had to say and did the job we came to do. On leaving my team went out while I was still in conversation with Minister Nicholas Ridley and on turning to go shook hands and opened the door and immediately disappeared into a large cupboard which I closed behind me. Embarrassment when arriving back in the room again, doesn't really sum it up.

In giving a presentation at a Probus meeting, I was conscious of a man in the centre of the room slowly keeling over. I knew I would never make it in time so I shouted a warning only to see the unfortunate guy crash to the floor apparently dead. What do you do after the ambulance has taken him away? Go on, wrap it up or what? I asked the audience what they wanted me to do; go on they said we were enjoying the story about Tommy Cooper. And I still got a few laughs even after that most unfortunate incident.

Like many others I used to use "overheads" and a large portable screen to assist talks, although today the power-point system has overtaken this method of visual displays. A few of my talks use power-point although I have rarely seen anyone else's work first time. I go over and over mine to make sure all is well – preparation being second nature to me. The amount of times I have been to professional marketing and promotional meetings where highly paid people struggle with their own equipment because the leads are not quite long enough, or the windows are in the wrong place for lighting purposes, or the hotel or whatever can't provide a high enough table etc, are too numerous to recall. The lesson is: prepare and always take all your own equipment.

Another lesson learned especially when children are around is NOT to ask the audience questions on the subject in hand. I well recall a talk on steam engines which got around to the subject of water when I asked: *'What liquid won't freeze?'* - *'Hot water'*, said an over brainy youngster.

Finally, arriving at a venue when you cannot get in is not fun. There is nothing worse than having to knock on the window of the room you are about to make "an entrance into" because someone has locked up too early.

Pat Fergusson and I went to grammar school in Skipton. Not actually the same school, because we were segregated - the girls school is 200 yards up the hill . We have been life-long friends and both of us have addressed a variety of audiences. Pat taught ceramics, changing direction to management training and latterly working as an English language lecturer in Manchester.

Now living on the Lancashire coast, Pat's love of language continues when she is called upon as a proof-reader, an increasingly unpopular yet essential role as punctuation and grammar are neither sexy nor greatly used as electronic communication takes over. She also dabbles in poetry writing, recently being published and viewing verse as a subtle way of evening scores instead of getting annoyed!

Home life includes active involvement with the women's group, Soroptimist International.

Warming up the Audience - Having listened to many types of delivery under the "Public Speaking" umbrella, it is clear there is no right or wrong way and the personality of the speakers matters far more than the subject. It's sad, then, that the most attractive subject can be made boring by a poor speaker but what may be perceived to be a dull topic can be transformed into the sort of presentation where afterwards you would follow the speaker to the far end of the earth, barefoot over broken glass!

Some speakers love to make contact with their audience before they begin and there are many ways how this can be done. I am sure that this is to calm the speaker's nerves as much as to put the audience at ease. Here are just a few that I have experienced.

"Would you mind slipping off your right shoe", suggested the speaker.

There was a little shuffling and then the speaker asked how many people had complied with his request. About 10% raised their hands.

"I'll ask you again. Would you mind slipping off a shoe, any one will do"

This time about 40% in total of the audience followed instructions.

It took a good five minutes for the audience to settle down and give the speaker their full attention again.

"Now, I asked you to do this because I am aware that however well-dressed you are, whatever level of management and how many of your colleagues are with you, you don't want to take off a shoe. Why? You may have a hole in your sock, your feet may smell and you may just look a little less like the image of yourself that you try to convey to your colleagues. It's a great leveller and I feel we are now bonded sufficiently for me to ascertain that most of my audience aren't half as scary as I thought they were when I first walked out onto this stage, especially the ones who never did take a shoe off. What do you have to hide? We'll never know".

Strengths - Introducing a course of work for the first time, I took along a colleague whom I knew always relied on the assumption that as I was younger and female, I would be perceived as his secretary; he enjoyed that when in fact the opposite was true and he was my subordinate, although older than me. I began the first session with an ice-breaker as the group of young men did not know each other and I wanted to put them at their ease.

"I'd like you to tell me something you are good at", I said, *"It can be anything, something about you personally which will tell me what you're like"* Asking this in the past had brought responses such as:

"I'm a good friend",

"I can make great scones",

"I love railway modelling and have nearly finished a model of Haworth Station which I began when I was eight"

"I can blow good smoke rings – but that's not clever as my Nan hates me smoking"

I suggested that my colleague started us off.

"Yes", he said, *"I'm proud to tell you that I have just achieved a first class honours degree".*

The room fell silent and nobody wanted to follow that.

About a year later, the same colleague told me he had used the same ice-breaker many times since then.

"After that day when I told them I'd got my degree, I realised what a self-inflated prat I must have looked to them because they all shut up, so now I tell them that I can double declutch and that gets the conversation going".

Things people tell you about Public Speaking - *"You don't get as nervous the longer you do it"* Not true, in my experience. As time goes on, you know how much more can go wrong.

"If you know your subject, you can wing it" Careful and thorough preparation is everything

"Just go as you are" Playing the game, wearing the suit, does count to make the audience know you care.

"Timing isn't important" Yes it is – vital. Find out how long you are expected to speak for and never, ever, go over it. Allow time for questions.

(This is also relevant to cultural differences as many nations believe that the more important you are, the longer you should speak for – regrettably, some people go on forever).

"I would never, ever speak in public. I can't do it" Yes, you can if you think it through. It will give you confidence and a voice that has every right to be heard

"Will you provide lecture notes? They're so useful, give relevant websites and further information."

Fine, until you see the next bloke pass the presentation and/or the notes off as his own.

It's happened to me and from the vague *"I've heard this before"* notion, to the realisation that somebody is freeloading and recycling your material, it does sound lame to complain when possibly the rest of the auditorium is enthralled. My material is still circulating years after my retirement. Bone idleness, on the part of the freeloader, or the sincerest form of flattery? Sad but true.

Conferences across the globe, meetings and study days held by the worldwide women's group Soroptimist International attract a range of illustrious and impressive speakers from politics, the media and the pertinent, public eye.

Around the world, Soroptimist International is known for almost a century of service, lobbying and being an active voice for, in particular, women and children. Over the years a variety of guests, from kitten-heeled politicians to bee-keeper-cum-news-readers, eminent medicos and professionals from all walks of life have been introduced, given their messages as diverse as the work of Soroptimist International itself, been applauded and thanked in a climate of supportive and generally appreciative equality.

Into this organised regime a well-known face was billed as main speaker, a popular and attractive man at the top of his game and whose daily presence was as familiar in our homes as our own family. His gravitas was marked by not one, but two women taking to the stage to acknowledge his achievements and welcome him.

He strode through the audience, even better looking in the flesh than on screen, suited, booted, smiling and melting female hearts with his ability to reach out to his audience. Yes, his presentation was efficient, interesting but not particularly rooted in the theme of the conference (for he had a book to sell), but hey! Those eyes! That smile! He could be excused a lacklustre patch when otherwise he was such a charming visual feast. How frail and fickle the faltering flesh sometimes, despite the solid Soroptimist objectives!

His presentation drew to a close and a Soroptimist sister took to the stage, the audience expecting that a senior officer would be called upon to present the final thanks and handshake. But no, she sashayed to the side of the presenter, took his arm and beamed towards the audience.

"I have been asked to proffer thanks and that's just what I'm going to do. On this occasion, ladies, sorry, but this one's for me".

Whereupon she moved in for the kill, encircled him with her arms and lifted her face to his, receiving from him a kiss and embrace which, I am sure, will have remained in her memory long after recriminations about her lapse in sisterly sharing, solidarity and equality were forgotten.

Pat also enjoys writing poetry so she offers some good poetic advice to any would-be speaker.

The Message Or:

"Tell them what you're going to tell them. Tell them again. Give them the message. Then tell them what you've told them"

Tell them what the message is, then tell them once again
Keep telling them your purpose because this is what they'll gain
Give them the presentation, your jokes, your treats, your tricks
Tell them the solution, if they are in a fix

Give them a Big Finish (a Shirley Bassey sort of way)
Remind them what your message is, of what you have to say
This telling, talking, telling, public speaking or conference call
Just leave them with a message or time is wasted. Wasted for us all.

Using Powerpoint: All Fur Coat and No Knickers

Up North, there's a saying, when trying to impress
Relating to decorum, as opposed to undress
Technology or tactics? Traditional or slicker?
The phrase is "wearing your fur coat, but never a knicker"

The laptop and powerpoint may seduce and delight, more or less
Introduce automation and lessen your stress
But you really can't beat the personal touch
Eye contact, good planning, all matter so much.

So next time you're tempted to a short techno cut
Go back to basics, not the easy-opt rut
Look right at your audience, no notes, crib or crutch
Stand tall and deliver – you owe them that much.

Rod Tuck, former elections advisor with the United Nations, local government officer and clerk for Newton Abbot Town Council, discovered one simple letter out of place caused him problems.

In October, 1989, whilst in the employment of the United Nations I was part of the election training team in Namibia. This was partly due to the fact that I had previously for 20 years been part of a team tutoring and lecturing electoral procedures in the United Kingdom.

The UN had invited 50 member countries to submit groups of civil servants and local government officers to act as election monitors across a large country where many of the local population were illiterate. My training base was in the North of Namibia at a 'high school' for girls. Needless to say, all pupils were on holiday so the large school hall could accommodate a classroom of several hundred visiting monitors. I could not believe it when I was in full flow with my lecture that a non-white gentleman in the audience stood up and shouted for me to stop until I could speak in the "*Queen's English*". My Ghanaian boss, who was a very senior member of the UN, asked me to continue but I must admit my confidence did suffer as a result of the interruption.

Back in the UK when giving my talk on Free and Fair Elections at one of the local clubs in a moorland town apparently the club's officers at the previous meeting had announced "*that our speaker next week will be Rod Tuck, subject 'Free and Fair Erections'*". There was a good turnout but one or two may have been a little disappointed when I talked about the democratic processes in Africa.

More recently at another local club the "apologies for absence" was higher than normal due to the fact that several considered that the same title of my talk *(Free and Fair Elections)* contradicted one of the aims of a Probus Club **that the club shall be .... and non political.**

Humour is a very useful asset in a talk and I did introduce at the University of the Third Age (U3A) one joke that a friend of one of our sons had submitted in a competition organised by BBC Radio Bristol two or three years ago and was topical. It concerned the exchange of prisoners between the USA and Russia. The USA handed over 12 Russians and Russia handed back 4 Americans. Why the difference in numbers? Answer: The exchange was carried out at a European airport and the combined weight of the four Americans equalled the weight of the 12 Russians.

A good friend is Merrilyn Williams who has given me plenty of encouragement to enjoy writing and public speaking. She writes under the pen names of Mel Menzies and Meg Scott and is the author of a number of books, one a number four bestseller. She is also Chairman of the National Association of Christian Writers (ACW) and blogs on her own website:

http://www.melmenzies.co.uk

I always say that when God was handing out the gift of a sense of direction, I was looking the wrong way! This has proved to be true on more than one occasion when I've been involved in public speaking. As the author of a number of books, I've had plenty of engagements arranged by my publishers; others requested by fans. Sometimes back to back, it can be tiring work. Even so...

I was travelling to a venue in North London one autumn evening, some years ago, when the train ground to a halt. An announcement from the train manager apologised for the delay and informed passengers that the reason was - wait for it - not leaves on the line, but cows on the line. In due course, it transpired that one had been hit and that we would be unable to resume our journey until the carcass was removed.

By the time we drew in to the railway station before my actual destination, which for some unknown reason we were unable to reach, it was dark. This was before the advent of mobile phones, and in this back-of-beyond station, there was one taxi and one telephone kiosk. I knew, in that moment, that I was not going to be the Before Dinner Speaker as booked, but the After Dinner - If At All - Speaker.

All was not lost, however. I managed to get both a message and a lift to the venue, dinner was delayed pending my arrival and I was, indeed, re-scheduled to be the After Dinner Speaker. Except...

Except that I knew I'd need a trip to the Ladies' Room before standing to address the venerable ladies and gentlemen gathered to hear about my latest book.

My host showed me the way, chatting all the time, then left me to it.

"*I have some notices to give out before you speak*," she said. "*See you back in the hall in a minute.*"

Well... That minute turned out to be nearer ten. The venue in which I was speaking was a sixth form college, and as anyone who has ever attended college will know, they are a maze of look-alike corridors. Engaged in conversation with my host on the way to the loo, I had not been concentrating on wither we went.

There was a slightly dazed expression on the face of my host when I eventually found my way back to the dinner table. But, true professional that I am, I turned it all to my advantage and, to the amusement of my audience, ad-libbed a redesigned opening for my talk on the subject of being lost and found.

Dan Erslan lives in a small town in Ohio. We met 30 years ago when he and his wife, Gail, lived near Boston. Since then there have been many trans-Atlantic visits. He is still active as a consultant in the rubber and plastics industry.

In High School I was on the 'announcing staff'. We had to produce and deliver the daily morning announcements over the school's public address system. We also produced the annual school talent show; a local radio personality emceed the shows. There came a point early in the show each year when we were to present a corsage to our advisor/home room teacher, Mrs. Upchurch. In one particular year it was my turn to present the corsage. The auditorium was packed with parents, friends and relatives of the various talent acts.

I came out in front of the curtain to the podium at the front of the stage and announced that we would like to invite Mrs. Upchurch to come to the stage. She must have been all the way in the back of the auditorium, and as I stood at the podium in the spotlight, having delivered my only line, I began to feel quite uncomfortable since it was taking her a long time to get to the stage. I remembered a line I had heard before, and thought it might be a way to break the silence. As I panned across the audience, straight-faced, I said: "I suppose you're all wondering why I've called this meeting." The line was well received and thankfully Mrs. Upchurch finally arrived. On with the show. Having no shame, I use that borrowed line frequently, even sometimes in crowded elevators!

One of my earliest jobs was as an apprentice electrician at The Goodyear Tire and Rubber Company. Goodyear had its corporate headquarters and many factories in Akron, Ohio, as did quite a few rubber companies. That was in the late 1960's. Goodyear had many excellent training programmes, two of which were their apprentice programme and their "Engineering Squadron" programme. As odd as it may sound, the apprentice programme was often a stepping stone toward a position in management.

The Engineering Squad was a two year programme to prepare candidates for supervisory or staff positions. There were several apprentice classes each year and at the end of the fourth year there was a graduation dinner. By the time our apprentice class graduation came around I was already on the Engineering Squad programme, and I was honoured to be asked to serve as emcee for the graduation programme and dinner. These dinners were usually attended by many of the corporation's top management. What an honour!

The keynote speaker that year was Russell DeYoung, Goodyear's Chairman of the Board of Directors. When I wasn't at the podium, I sat next to him throughout dinner and the programme. My mother and father were also at the table with me. I was so proud, as were they. I don't remember much of the detail, but apparently I did an excellent job, because I received several letter from members of upper management telling me just that.

Within seven years of starting the apprentice programme I was named The Manager of Engineering and Maintenance at a Goodyear factory in north western Ohio, which set the stage for my entire career.

I am certain that one speaking engagement wasn't the only reason for my rise in the company, but it surely didn't hurt. How very fortunate I have been.

Speaking to a multicultural audience is summed up by these two stories which illustrate how cultural differences can often distract a speaker unprepared for something outside their experience – up to now. The author, a teacher, prefers to remain anonymous.

First story - I used the first session of the new academic year to outline expectations: the timetable, the syllabus, deadlines, coursework and examinations so that there should be complete understanding between me and my students. About 30 students took their seats in the lecture theatre, ranging from a sole male centrally on the front row, in twos and threes up the tiers until the inevitable rebels on the back row.

I enjoyed meeting my students for the first time, interested to see who took advantage of the opportunity for questions and comparing my first impressions with their performance as the year progressed. The first hour of the weekly three hour session, on this occasion, gave no interruptions as I explained the pleasures and the pitfalls awaiting the students, inevitably a varied bunch, straight-out-of-school or of more mature age, smart, casual, a complete melting pot of shapes, sizes and situations.

After sweeping the room with my gaze gathering general impressions, I became aware of a constant slight movement on the front row where a smart, dark man, a more mature student, sat alone, as close as any student could be to me. His fingers fiddled with his nose, his ears, his mouth and I was appalled to realise that he was excavating every orifice and transferring the contents to his mouth. I made an urgent mental note to have a word with the student's Personal Tutor, whom I knew to be a man of discretion who would be able to discourage such unpleasant habits.

The session continued. The fiddling continued. Suddenly, a jackpot haul of huge proportions emerged from the man's nose and was transferred on his finger to his mouth........I paused, distracted and horrified and without thinking of my previous intentions to be discreet, hissed quietly but clearly, *"For goodness sake, would you please stop doing that. If you must, use a handkerchief"*.

"Why?" responded the student, *"Have I got strings?"* he said, touching his nose from which he obviously thought something more was emerging.

With as little upheaval and embarrassment as possible, I asked the student to go to the men's cloakrooms to conclude his "grooming" and without this extreme in-house entertainment, the lecture continued with no further interruption.

The Personal Tutor successfully discouraged future displays of a similar kind but the student, who was called Hamid, and had recently come to Manchester from North Africa, continued to sit on his own and did not mix with the other students.

After the Christmas recess, Hamid arrived at his first lecture of the new term wearing a brightly checked woollen coat, double breasted and ideal for the cold of that particular January. It seemed that he had wisely and thriftily visited a charity shop for warm clothes to protect against his first British winter. He was snugly buttoned into his coat and again took his place on the front row.

An hour or so later, sweat poured from his brow, he looked most hot and uncomfortable, shifting in his seat but never loosening his coat.

"Why don't you take your coat off, Hamid?" I asked.

There was a long pause and then Hamid's face lit up.

"May I?" he asked.

It was obvious that he had sensibly bought warm clothes but thought it to be rude and disrespectful to remove one's clothing in a public place.

Hamid settled to student life but tested the boundaries of staff-student relations by ardently pursuing a young lecturer who, like himself, was married with a family. She swiftly discouraged his advances which, I believe, he put down to "British Reserve" rather than the cultural differences which were the real reason behind his behaviour; not wrong, just different.

Second story - In rural China the Supervisor came every Monday to check on the progress of the mature students who were learning English at a remote and rural Chinese school. She was English and spent the morning with the students and their teacher, all of them Chinese, but appreciating the input of a "real English person" on a weekly basis.

The format was much the same every week. The Supervisor arrived early and looked at the written work and checked that the course syllabus was being followed. The students arrived and were given a talk of about an hour and a half, the subject related to life and culture in Britain; a notably long time for either The Supervisor to talk or the students to sit still and listen as there was no break in the proceedings, but that was the way it was done.

On her first visit, The Supervisor was astonished at the extreme isolation of the school room, which was little more than a shed in a clearing, having an earth floor and few amenities beyond desks and chairs. She met the teacher, made checks of the paperwork, registers and workbooks, then met the pupils as they silently filed into their seats.

The simple surroundings were a marked contrast to the formality of the teaching and the regular teacher sat to one side, the pupils still and compliant behind desks whilst The Supervisor delivered her talk.

Recalling these sessions afterwards, The Supervisor said that she was aware of an odd, low grumbling noise which she could not identify and the only movement in the room was each pupil's throat contracting and pulsing as their eyes became wider, unblinking, but were still fixed on her at the front of the room.

After perhaps half an hour, suddenly one pupil leaned quickly to one side and cleared the phlegm which he had gradually worked up into his throat and emitted it in an enormous blob of spittle onto the earth floor, resuming then the benign gaze and open-eyed attention to The Supervisor.

This unleashed identical spitting and clearing of the throat by every student, a feature of Chinese daily morning behaviour practised nationally at that time "to clear the tubes".

The Supervisor remained in her position at the front of the class, fearing that to walk amongst the desks she would encounter slimy deposits of such proportions that she would soil her shoes and possibly slip and fall.

Subsequent visits repeated the throat clearing, eye goggling routine and The Supervisor tried to change the timetable so that the students could clear their throats before her talk, but this never worked as it seemed to be the quiet, still atmosphere which enabled the pupils to concentrate on this daily habit. The earth floor was never swept or sanitised and the stains remained.

Relating this tale much later, The Supervisor considered how larger schools would have been organised. She knew of no use of spittoons and hard flooring would have been more of a problem than the earth floor of the schoolroom of her experience. She did say that as she became used to this quiet interruption, the back ground sounds of gentle rumbling noises were part of the atmosphere and recognised that this was part of the culture of the country.

Christine Morey is typical of thousands of people in the UK who give up their free time to talk to a variety of local organisations. First of all, though, she had to get her message across via different translators.

I have always found it easy to talk to and teach people who are keen to learn. I had never done any public speaking as such until June 1991 when I set off for Romania to teach women how to start their own small business using hand driven knitting machines.

Computerised knitting machines had taken over in the UK making the hand driven ones redundant, but in a training centre in Brasov were five unused Swiss machines just waiting for someone to come along and teach the locals how to use them.

I had my own Residential Knitting Machine School in Paignton but when on television I saw the poverty in Romania I slowly began to realise that somehow I might be able to help.

I arrived late at night to discover the car that was supposed to take me into the city – a two and a half hour drive away – had not turned up. I persuaded a taxi driver to take me only to find that when I arrived at my hotel in the early hours of the morning there was no room booked in my name. It was a nerve-wracking start. Things didn't get much easier when I eventually found my way to the training centre and discovered there was no translator. My first public speaking engagement involved me learning a new skill – sign language. I became quite adept it at over the next few days.

Later in the week I learnt that some of the teachers at the training centre had initially thought I had come to steal their valuable knitting machines because they had been brain-washed into believing that nobody from Britain would go to Romania unless it was for something they could get their hands on! Even then I had to spend three hours speaking through an interpreter before I could convince the people who ran the Training Centre that the women should be taught by an English woman rather than a Swiss.

It was the start of an adventure which took me back to Romania many times over the next few years and then on to Lithuania, Ukraine, India, Kenya, Ghana and Tajikistan teaching women how to use the knitting machines and make a living. Over a 15 year period I managed to get my hands on around 1,200 machines which were no longer needed here and ship them out to these countries.

Back in England I was invited to talk about my experiences to local rotary, probus and ladies groups. This enabled me to raise awareness and, in some cases, raise the money to keep the project going. I wasn't a professional speaker but I knew what I wanted to say and since my first such talk I have never relied on notes or used an overhead projector. I speak from the heart for about 40 minutes and then invite questions. I don't feel nervous when I get up to speak and just try and be myself.

In recent years I have become a Street Pastor and have spoken to many of the same organisations about the excellent work we do to reduce tensions and problems late at night near local entertainment hot spots in Torbay.

I am a member of Paignton Ladies Group and the Torbay Ladies Luncheon Club. Some speakers are excellent and a few dreadful. The best speaker I have heard was a vicar's wife who collected Victorian underwear. She captivated her audience talking about some of the incredible items she had collected.

Another speaker who gives a lot of his spare time to address local organisations is historian John Risden.

I am indeed fortunate in that I love my craft, that being lecturing on the diverse subject of local heritage. Experience has given me confidence in what I do and the fact that I ENJOY sharing my knowledge with others. Two pieces of advice I give to others wishing to participate in public speaking are:-

1. Prepare your subject in advance with objectives, but don't simply try to learn it off by heart.

2. Take your time, speak clearly and with confidence.

UKIP councillor Julien Parrott was plunged into a hectic speaking schedule when he became chairman of Torbay Council in 2013, but it was a talk he gave in Belfast which he remembers the most.

In my experience successful speeches always involve something that you feel passionate about. The only rule then is to 'know your audience'. I have delivered 'tub-thumping' political speeches to the party-faithful, speeches to industry, and, as chairman of the council, to an exceedingly diverse range of groups including ex drug addicts, war veterans, young people at awards ceremonies, chess champions and Miss England contestants and organisers!

Strange to think that I felt passionate about all of these things - the link being a passion for the people and success of our Bay (I feel a speech coming on even as I write!!).

However, the most successful speech I think have ever given was to around five or six hundred construction professionals and guests at a conference in Belfast for the, then, Institute of Building Control. The conference was to be the very last for the Institute as it was about to merge with the Royal Institution of Chartered Surveyors (and thereby gain treasured royal chartered status for the members).

As the Chief Executive of the Institute, I was effectively saying goodbye and good luck to all the members that I had been honoured to serve. I also felt the need to urge them to fight hard for their profession as they moved into a very much larger organisation with a world-wide membership.

For that reason I had only one slide for my presentation in the very large conference hall - the crest of the Institute of Building Control. It is sufficient to say that by the end of the speech the members, a good few in tears, were truly fired up and excited by the thoughts that I had shared. The speech and the lunch afterwards was something that I will never forget.

The thought that I would most like to share with any reader is that, while public speaking is hard-work, stressful and, depending on the audience, not a little scary, it is important to remember that it is always a privilege to be listened to by others.

CHAPTER SIX

ON THE

LOOKOUT

True fame is when the newspapers spell your name right in Karachi –
football manager Brian Clough

An incredible amount of work and effort goes into finding speakers for the many clubs and organisations seeking some entertainment once the business part of their meetings is over. Speakers are normally booked well in advance so the club can get its annual programme down in writing for all to see – and so its members can decide which meetings they want to attend and those they may wish to avoid.

From my experience a speaking engagement usually starts with an exploratory telephone call to see if I am available, whether I am willing to travel and what I charge. Once the details are agreed I usually get a confirmation letter either in the post or by email, followed by a telephone call a few days before to check I have not forgotten, but probably to ensure I am still alive!

Some organisations have speaker-finders meetings where clubs in a given geographical area send their man or woman to try and unearth new speakers and discuss the merits or otherwise of inviting someone. Some speakers are 'blackballed' at these meetings if they have not come up to scratch.

On several occasions I have been asked to speak at the last minute when someone has fallen ill. One speaker secretary telephoned to enquire whether I could speak the next day at his club meeting. *"Our members have been keen to hear you speak for some time, "* he said. *' I am so glad you can step in because you are the eighth person I have rung this morning."*

This chapter is a fitting finale and is dedicated to those who give up their free time to get people like me to entertain them. They deserve greater recognition and praise than they often receive.

Ken Browse was speaker-finder for the Rotary Club of Paignton for six years and had to find a different speaker every two weeks; no easy task. I have been invited to speak to the club on three occasions – recognition indeed! Ken searched far and wide for speakers on different topics.

I used to listen to 'Pause for Thought' every morning on Radio Devon and if I found someone spoke well for the few minutes allotted them, I would give them a call to see if they would come and speak to my members. Very few people turned down the invitation.

As a speaker-finder you do feel personally responsible and hope that everyone enjoys each meeting. Mind you, we do have some members who enjoy a bit of fun when it comes to the question and answer sessions. When the Rev David Coffey came he told us how uncomfortable he felt on a visit to the Soviet Union in the 1980s when every bus had two men in long black coats watching passengers. One of our members stood up and tongue in cheek asked: *'Would we solve our unemployment problems if two men in black coats travelled on the back of all our buses!?'*

Some speakers are more memorable than others. Benny Goodman (not THE Benny Goodman) was a wing commander in the Second

World War who flew one of the planes that dropped thousands of bombs on Dresden in 1944. It was one of the most controversial raids of the war. Benny was just 24 at the time. In later life he became a well known faith healer in Kingsbridge and he gave us a moving talk on 'From Killing to Healing'.

One day I was working at the crab factory I owned when the High Sheriff of Devon Sir Simon Day called in to buy a case of crab meat. He said he had heard on the grapevine our product was the best in the business. I persuaded him to come and speak to our club, which he duly did in the poshest accent of anyone we had ever heard. One of our members commented afterwards: "*I never thought people liked that existed!*"

Embarrassing moments have, fortunately, been few and far between, but at one meeting we double booked a guest speaker and the then Rotary district governor, who was not the best of entertainers. We always have a good lunch before introducing the speaker and when the district governor had not arrived by the start of the meal we assumed he would not be coming after all. Our president duly got up to introduce the outside speaker and said: "*You have been saved from having to listen to our district governor because he has not turned up as expected.*" However, he had slipped in at the back unnoticed by most people. He stayed silent.

Some speakers think that because they are speaking to an all-male audience they can litter their talk with crude, sexual jokes. Two supposedly professional businessmen who came to our club met with no more than polite applause when they treated us as though we were a bunch of dirty old men. They totally mis-read their audience and were not funny.

We have been fortunate over the years in attracting some good local speakers and some celebrities. Sir Ranulph Fiennes read out his school report which said .....' *this boy is going nowhere!*', while Commander Chris Wreford-Brown, in command of the submarine

HMS Conqueror during the Falklands War, told us how he was given permission by Prime Minister Margaret Thatcher to sink the Argentine cruiser the General Belgrano.

I also enjoyed talks by astronomer Patrick Moore, Dr David Bellamy and local woman Debra Veale who set off with her husband to row 3,000 miles across the Atlantic. He quit after eight days but she carried on for another 103 days and made it to Barbados. She is an exceptional woman.

One of the most entertaining speakers was the late David Penhaligon, the Liberal MP for Truro. He was the guest speaker at Rotary's South West Conference and he kept everyone amused with his Cornish stories and particularly those while canvassing during a General Election. He knocked on one door and was assured he had the man's vote, but as he left he was asked: ' *Where is this Europe they keep going on about?* ' Realising the man was deadly serious, David replied: ' *Don't worry, it's the other side of the Tamar'*.

I have heard many jokes over the years but one of the best was the story of folk who were trying to put their family tree together. The problem was they knew there was a black sheep in the family – an Uncle George who years earlier had been electrocuted in the electric chair for murdering someone. This was a deep embarrassment to all of them. They didn't want people to know about it and told the biographer about their worries. He told them not to worry because he would handle it sensitively and not cause them any embarrassment. True to his word the biographer wrote: 'Uncle George occupied a chair of applied electronics at an important government institution. He was attached to this position by the strongest of ties and his death came as a real shock.'

Peggy Bradley has been speaker-finder for both Torbay Women's Luncheon Club and Paignton Ladies Group. Both groups meet monthly – the Luncheon Club on the first Tuesday each month and the Ladies Group on the second Monday.

It is a lovely, but stressful job. I have done it for at least 12 years on and off. If anyone is thinking of taking on the job on behalf of their organisation I have six useful tips.

1. If at all possible go somewhere to hear the proposed speaker for yourself. If not try and find out if someone you know has heard him or her and ask whether they would recommend them.
2. Always know your speaker's requirements, whether it be a screen, table or other equipment. Not every lead is long enough.
3. Never forget to have a jug of water and glass available for the speaker.
4. Make sure there are no misunderstandings about the fee.
5. Educate your speaker about the audience they can expect.
6. If you want them to do a good job, you have to look after them. Always give a warm welcome and never leave them on their own in the coffee period before the start.

I have enjoyed hosting several speakers the night before. It saves the club the expense of paying for dinner/bed and breakfast at a nearby hotel and gives me the chance to brief the speaker about what we expect. It also means I know they will be there on time on the day. Over the years only one speaker failed to turn up and that was because he was coming by train and got held up by snow.

I always have a reserve list of speakers I can call upon at the last minute and, in a real emergency, I know I can step in and speak myself if required.

The Luncheon Club aim to have two high profile speakers a year who charge large fees, otherwise we pay anything up to £50 per speaker which usually covers their expenses.

I have heard some lovely talks and have particularly enjoyed those by ordinary people who have done something interesting or are interesting themselves. One speaker said his subject was 'Feet First' and this left some of our ladies baffled when our annual programme was published. They came to me and wanted to know more, but I decided to keep them in the dark until the actual day. When he arrived he was in his late fifties and was a thalidomide baby. Thalidomide was given to pregnant women in the 1950s and early 1960s to combat morning sickness but led to children being born without limbs. He had no arms but he demonstrated how he used a knife and fork and how he could do other things I take for granted. He was married with two grown up children and gave us a captivating talk. He said people assumed he wouldn't be capable, but he had proved how wrong they were.

I was fortunate because although he lived not far away in Dawlish he had not given his talk in my area before. It wasn't always possible to get speakers nobody had heard, but I did try.

I think we have been fortunate in the quality of our speakers, but we did have one disaster when I had to step in and end the 'entertainment'. From the moment I met him I just knew he was not right for our club. I chatted to him throughout the lunch and I became more fearful as time went by. He came to talk about letters written by his parents during the First World War and behind his chair he had a huge pile of papers. He would talk for a few moments then turn his back on the audience while he hunted for the appropriate letter, sometimes muttering that he could not find it. I could tell the audience was not enjoying it so I started looking at my watch every minute as he rambled on and on without saying much of interest. Eventually I interrupted and said that we only had the room for a set amount of time so could he draw his talk to a conclusion. He seemed most put out and still went on for another ten minutes oblivious to the lack of reaction he was getting from his audience. I am glad to say it is the only time I have ever curtailed somebody's talk.

Wendy John is the former deputy head teacher at Churston Grammar School and now has the job of finding regular speakers for a Monday Lunch Club for the over 65s at Upton Vale Baptist Church.

I have not done much public speaking myself, but when I was head of English at Devonport School for Girls I was asked to give a talk on 'any theme about Shakespeare'. I chose to talk about Shakespeare and Love and it seemed to go down well with the 50 or so people present.

I am currently putting together a talk on nursery rhymes. People don't realise how scary some of the rhymes really are and how many of them have a sad ending, like Humpty Dumpty and Rock-a-bye-Baby. I am enjoying doing the research prior to giving the talk.

When I was deputy head teacher I had the job of finding speakers for our annual speech day. I did this for 15 years and spent a lot of time studying what was going on in the world and trying to get a topical speaker from business, politics or sport. One year we were doing a major environmental project so I got Sir Tim Smit, co-founder of the Eden Project, to come and he gave a fascinating and much appreciated talk.

I was only sorry we did not have any high profile speakers in our local area I could call upon.

The Monday Lunch Club caters for about 70 people aged 65 and over. They get a three course lunch after which we either have a speaker or some entertainment. I try and offer a mixed programme because I know many of those present like a good old sing-song sometimes. We have a pianist some weeks who is good at meeting any request.

We have a 'Thought for the Day' session and then I ask the guest speaker to talk for around 30 minutes; I tell them not to worry if they over-run a bit, particularly those who bring slides. We give people a chance to ask questions afterwards and that is always a sign of how interested they have been in what the speaker has had to say.

I find the best speakers are those who speak with some passion about their chosen subject.

Two tips I would like to give would-be speaker-finders is to network with other speaker finders in their area and read the local newspaper. I listen to what friends have to say when they have heard somebody speak at the museum or at a Rotary or WI meeting. The newspaper has a weekly 'clubs news' section which names speakers and their subjects.

Jim Biggs is speaker-finder for Dartmouth Probus Club.

I recall an occasion which was not a disaster but certainly a delight tinged with sadness.

Many years ago (early 1970s) I went to a Round Table function in Essex and after dinner the principal guest was introduced – a surgeon named Arthur Dixon-Wright – who started off as a very boring speaker and I wondered how long we should have to put up with him. Within minutes though he had turned round the focus of his talk to his experiences as a surgeon to the nobility.

It was embellished in places but his audience was like putty in his hands. His humour left us totally out of control of our senses and with exceedingly painful and side splitting consequences – one lady at the dinner gave premature birth the following day! Dickson-Wright was then considered one of the top six after dinner speakers and this was my first encounter - never to be forgotten.

Later on, circa 1975, I approached him to come to a dinner meeting I was organising to which he agreed to do for the princely sum of £100 as a donation to the Imperial Cancer Fund. All I had by way of confirmation was a post card saying *'delighted to come to your event if I am still alive'*. A few days before the dinner in February 1976, I had a call from his daughter, Clarissa (one of the two Fat Ladies) who very sadly told me that *'he would not be able to come to our event as he had just died in Cairo, where he usually spent the winters, and was very sorry!!'*

So my second encounter never happened but the memories are as vivid now as they were that night in Essex – the story of the Duchess and her constipation and many others. I still laugh about it now and fondly remember the man.

Another Probus Club speaker-finder until the end of 2013 was Roger Frost. He reveals his biggest worry was ensuring the allotted speaker turned up on the right day and at the right time.

Like most clubs we book our speakers well in advance. For one meeting we had a naval officer coming from Portsmouth to speak on *'The role of saving the realm'*. Trying to contact him was impossible because the address he had given us had changed and nobody knew where he was. Fortunately I found a leaflet he had sent many months before and on it was a telephone number which enabled me to track him down. He duly turned up on time and gave an excellent talk.

On another occasion I was worried when all attempts to contact our next speaker by telephone failed. I went to his house to find it all locked up so I left a note on the door. Apparently he was on holiday until only a few hours before he was due to speak to us, but all's well that ends well because he turned up on time.

There was always the fear at the back of my mind that the speaker would not make it, either through mixing up the dates or illness, so I ensured I had a back-up available whom I could call upon in an emergency.

Probus clubs are non political but some members can also be touchy if they think someone is trying to use their talk to sell something. I had a very good solicitor come and give an excellent talk about wills, but it did not go down well with a few who thought he was trying to drum up business. The same thing happened when we had an insurance expert give an insight into his work.

It goes to prove the old saying that you can't please all of the people all of the time.

John Skirton is speaker-finder for both Coleridge Probus Club and Prawle Point Coastwatch.

When I joined the Probus Club I was given two options: become vice chairman or speaker-finder. I opted for the latter and by and large I enjoy the job. The club meets on the second Wednesday of every month and after some business at the start of our meetings we invite a speaker to entertain and inform us for around 45 minutes.

We are part of the South Devon Speakers' Circle which meets three times a year. Speaker-finders have to come to these meetings with three speakers they recommend after which a list is circulated to every club. Then it is up to them who they invite. It is not unusual for some speakers to be recommended several times at the same meeting.

We try and get a variety of speakers and have invited some people back a second time, although on one occasion we discovered that while the speaker first time round was excellent, he was very poor the second time he came to us.

My wife is a speaker-finder for the WI so we compare notes and help each other, but I have noticed it is getting more difficult because of travel costs.

I always contact the speaker a week before our meetings and I am fortunate in that within our club we have two members who can always step in at the last moment if anyone falls ill.

One memorable speaker brought his identical twin brother. They really did look alike and it wasn't until one of them stood up to talk about 'Forays of a Pharmacist' that we really knew who was who. They were both top class fencers.

After we give a vote of thanks to the speaker new members are asked in advance to give a five minute talk about themselves. One man had to be stopped by the chairman when he rambled on for more than 20 minutes. At that point he had only reached what he was doing when aged 26!

CHAPTER SEVEN

JOKES FOR

THE TELLING

If at first you don't succeed, don't try sky diving! – unknown comedian

A bagpiper was asked by a funeral director to play at a graveside service for a homeless man. He had no family or friends, so the service was to be at a pauper's cemetery in the Nova Scotia back country.

As he was not familiar with the backwoods, he got lost and, being a typical man, he didn't stop for directions.

He finally arrived an hour late and saw the funeral guy had evidently gone and the hearse was nowhere in sight. There were only the diggers and crew left and they were eating lunch. He felt badly and apologized to the men for being late.

He went to the side of the grave and looked down and saw the vault lid was already in place. He didn't know what else to do, so I started to play. The workers put down their lunches and began to gather around.

He played out his heart and soul for this man with no family and friends like he had never played before. And as he played "Amazing Grace" the workers began to weep. They wept, he wept, they all wept together. When he finished, he packed up his bagpipes and started for his car. Though his head was hung low, his heart was full.

As he opened the door to his car, he heard one of the workers say, "I have never seen nothing like that before and I've been putting in septic tanks for 20 years."

Apparently, it's a man thing.

A woman visited a Northern newspaper to place a bereavement notice following the death of her husband. 'How much?' she asked the girl at the counter and was told it was 20p a word. She was not happy and went to a desk to write out what she wanted to say on an official form. When she had finished she handed in the form and 60p. All it said was: ' Murgatroyd is dead'. The receptionist had the difficult job of telling her there was a minimum charge of £1.20 for six words. The woman was deeply unhappy at this news and snatched back the form. She dipped into her purse for another 60p and wrote on the form ' Murgatroyd is dead. Volvo for sale.'

One daily newspaper asked its readers 'what it means to be British?' The best reply came from a man in Switzerland who wrote: ' Being British is about driving in a German car to an Irish pub for a Belgian beer, then travelling home, grabbing an Indian curry or a Turkish kebab on the way, to sit on Swedish furniture and watch American shows on a Japanese television. And the most British thing of all? Suspicion of anything foreign.'

A priest was being honoured at his retirement dinner after 25 years in the parish. The local newspaper editor and a member of the congregation were chosen to make the presentation and give a short speech at the dinner. He was delayed, so the priest decided to say his own few words while they waited. ' I got my first impression of the parish from the first confession I heard here. I thought I had been assigned to a terrible place.

' The very first person who entered my confessional told me he had stolen a television set and, when questioned by the police was able to lie his way out of it. He had stolen money from his parents, embezzled from his employer, had an affair with his boss's wife and taken illegal drugs. I was appalled, but as the days went on I knew that my people were not at all like that and I had, indeed, come to a fine parish full of good and loving people.'

Just as the priest finished his talk the editor arrived full of apologies at being late. He immediately began to make the presentation and gave his talk. ' I'll never forget the first day our parish priest arrived, said the editor. ' In fact I had the honour of being the first person to go to him for confession!!'

A surgeon, a general and a newspaper editor were in the same first class carriage on a train between Devon and London. They began to debate which was the oldest profession in the world and agreed to use the Bible as their guide.

'Mine must be,' said the surgeon,' because it says in the Bible that woman was made from man's rib and who could do that but a surgeon?'

'Nonsense,' said the general. ' If you are going to quote the Bible then mine must be the oldest profession because before then it says that order was created out of chaos.'

'Ah,' said the editor, 'but who do you think created the chaos in the first place?'

After a tiring day visiting company headquarters in London for yet another boring meeting a newspaper editor settled down in his seat on the train back home and closed his eyes. As the train rolled out of the station, the young woman sitting next to him pulled out her cell phone and started talking in a loud voice:
"Hi sweetheart. It's Sue. I'm on the train".
"Yes, I know it's the six thirty and not the four thirty, but I had a long meeting".
"No, honey, not with that Kevin from the accounting office. It was with the boss".
"No sweetheart, you're the only one in my life".
"Yes, I'm sure, cross my heart!"
Fifteen minutes later, she was still talking loudly.
When the editor had had enough, he leaned over and said into the phone: "Sue, hang up the phone and come back to bed."
Sue doesn't use her cell phone in public any longer.

One very rich newspaper owner bought a huge farm and invited some of his senior managers to have a look round followed by lunch. After touring some of the 1,500 acres of land, rivers and hills he took everyone back to the house, which was as spectacular as the scenery. Behind the house was a large swimming pool. There was just one thing unusual though – it contained two crocodiles.

The newspaper owner explained that he valued courage among his managers more than any other trait and that was what had made him a multi millionaire. ' In fact, ' he said ' courage is such a powerful virtue that if anyone is courageous enough to jump in the pool, swim through those crocodiles and make it to the other side, I will give them either £20,000, a new car, or the holiday of a lifetime.'

Of course everyone laughed at such an absurd challenge and proceeded to follow the owner into the house for lunch. Suddenly they heard a splash and turning round they saw a young man swimming for his life across the pool. The crocodiles closed in but he managed to pull himself out of the water at the far end unharmed.

The rich host applauded his efforts and stuck to his promise. He said to the dripping wet manager: ' Tell me what you want - £20,000, a car or a holiday?' The young swimmer breathed heavily for a moment, looked up at his host and said: ' I want to know just one thing. Who the hell pushed me into that pool?'

Proposed cuts to the NHS (National Health Service) services (or lack of them)!

The BMA (British Medical Association) has weighed in on the Prime Minister's new health care proposals.

The Allergists voted to scratch it, but the Dermatologists advised not to make any rash moves.

The Gastroenterologists had a sort of a gut feeling about it, but the neurologists thought the Administration had a lot of nerve.
The Obstetricians felt they were all labouring under a misconception.

Ophthalmologists considered the idea short-sighted.

Pathologists yelled, "Over my dead body!" while the Paediatricians said, "Oh, Grow up!"

The Psychiatrists thought the whole idea was madness, while the Radiologists could see right through it.

The Surgeons were fed up with the cuts and decided to wash their hands of the whole thing.

The ENT specialists didn't swallow it, and just wouldn't hear of it.

The Pharmacologists thought it was a bitter pill to swallow, and the Plastic Surgeons said, "This puts a whole new face on the matter....."

The Podiatrists thought it was a step forward.

The Anaesthetists thought the whole idea was a gas, but needed to sleep on it.

A lawyer and an elderly man are sitting next to each other on a long flight. The lawyer is thinking that old people are so dumb that he could get one over on them easily. So he asks if the man would like to play a fun game.

The man is tired and just wants to take a nap, so he politely declines and tries to catch a few winks.

The lawyer persists, saying that the game is a lot of fun...."I ask you a question, and if you don't know the answer, you pay me only £5. Then you ask me one, and if I don't know the answer, I will pay you

£500," he says. This catches the old man's attention and, to keep the lawyer quiet, he agrees to play the game.

The lawyer asks the first question. "What's the distance from the Earth to the Moon?" The old man doesn't say a word, but reaches into his pocket, pulls out a five pound note, and hands it to the lawyer.

Now, it's his turn. He asks the lawyer, "What goes up a hill with three legs, and comes down with four?" The lawyer uses his laptop to search all references he can find on the Net. He sends e-mails to all the smart friends he knows; all to no avail. After an hour of searching, he finally gives up.

He wakes the senior and hands him £500. The old man pockets the £500 and goes right back to sleep. The lawyer is going nuts not knowing the answer. He wakes the man up and asks, "Well, so what goes up a hill with three legs and comes down with four?" The older man reaches into his pocket, hands the lawyer £5, and goes back to sleep.

An elderly couple were having dinner one evening when the husband reached across the table, took his wife's hand in his and said:' Mary soon we will be married for 50 years and there's something I have to know. In all these 50 years, have you ever been unfaithful to me?'

Mary replied: 'Well Henry, I have to be honest with you. Yes I have been unfaithful three times during those 50 years, but always for a good reason.

Henry was obviously hurt by his wife's confession. ' I never suspected. Can you tell me what you mean by "good reasons" ?'.

So Mary told him the first time was shortly after they married and were about to lose their house because they couldn't afford the mortgage. ' Do you remember that one evening I went to see the bank manager and the next day he notified you that the loan would be extended?'

Henry recalled the visit and said: 'I can forgive you that, you saved our home, but what about the second time?'

Mary recalled the time Henry was sick but didn't have the money to go private and have heart surgery. ' Well, I went to see the surgeon one night and, if you remember, he did the surgery at no charge.'

'I remember that too,' admitted Henry. ' It probably saved my life so of course I can forgive you for that as well. Now tell me about the third.' 'All right,' said Mary. ' So do you remember when you ran for president of your golf club and you needed 73 more votes?'

One day a florist went to his local barber for a haircut. After the cut he asked 'how much?' and the barber replied: ' I cannot accept any money from you because I am doing community service this week. The florist was pleased. The next morning when the barber went to open his shop there was a 'thank you' card and a dozen roses waiting in the doorway.

Later a policeman came in for a haircut and when he tried to pay he was also told there would not be a charge because of the community service order. The next morning when the barber went to open up there was another 'thank you' card and a dozen doughnuts.

That day a councillor came in for a haircut and he too was told he didn't have to pay anything. The next day when the barber went to open up a dozen councillors were lined up waiting for a free haircut.

One well known public speaker never touched any food or drink before getting up to address his audience and always relied on his wife to leave him a sandwich and drink in the kitchen for when he got home. One night after addressing a rotary club he arrived home to find the table empty. Puzzled, he went to the fridge and on the floor noticed a basket which contained five eggs and £1,000. He went up to the bedroom and enquired of his wife what the eggs and money meant. ' Ah,' she said,' in this town I am given an egg every time you give a bad talk.' 'And the £1,000?' he asked. ' Oh, when I get a dozen I sell them and that's the proceeds.'

A thief called Archie attacked an elderly woman in Tescos, throttled her and grabbed her purse. Inside was just 50p. As he was leaving he spotted another frail pensioner and attacked her as well. Again there was just 50p in her purse. The headline next day in the local paper read: *Archie chokes two for 50p in Tescos!*

An 80-year-old man went to the doctor for a checkup and the doctor was amazed at what good shape the guy was in. The doctor asked: ' To what do you attribute your good health?' The old timer said: ' I'm a golfer and that's why I am in such good shape. I'm up well before daylight and out up and down the fairways.

The doctor felt there was more to his good health than that so he probed a bit more: ' Well I am sure that helps. How old was your father when he died?' 'Who said my father's dead?' came the retort.

Intrigued the doctor asked: ' You mean you are 80 years old and your father is still alive? How old is he?' The old timer said: ' He's 101 years old actually and, in fact, he golfed with me this morning. That's why he is still alive – he's a golfer'

The doctor still wasn't satisfied that he had found the real answer to the man's good health so he said: ' How about your grandfather. How old was he when he died?' The reply was the same: ' Who said he is dead?'

'You mean you are 80 years old and your grandfather's still living? How old is he?' The golfer said: ' He's 118 years old.'

The doctor was getting frustrated at this point and said: ' I guess he went golfing with you too this morning'?' ' No, grandpa couldn't go this morning because he got married.'

The doctor said in amazement: ' Got married! Why would a 118-year-old man want to get married?'

'Who said he wanted to? 'said the old boy.

Eleven people were hanging on a rope under a helicopter – ten men and one woman. The rope wasn't strong enough to carry them all, so they decided that one person had to leave because otherwise they were all going to fall. They weren't able to decide who that person should be until the woman gave a very touching speech. She said she would voluntarily let go of the rope because, as a woman, she was used to giving up everything for her husband, kids and men in general. As soon as she finished her speech, all the men started clapping!

An old Yorkshireman's wife dies and because she was a God-fearing Baptist and regular church-goer, he orders a headstone for her with the words: ' *She was thine'*. Unfortunately when he goes to collect and pay for it, the headstone says: ' *She was thin'*.

'What about the "e",' he complains. The stonemason was most apologetic and promised to correct it within 24 hours. Next day the Yorkshireman went back to collect the headstone to find it now said:' *E, she was thin'*.

A Hindu, Muslim and a UK MP found themselves stranded when their flight from the Middle East was cancelled and the only hotel anywhere near had just one twin bedded room available. The Hindu offered to sleep in the stable at the back, but returned within five minutes because there was a cow inside . The Muslim said he would sleep in the stable but he was back also within five minutes when he discovered a pig. The politician reluctantly agreed to sleep in the stable. Within five minutes the cow and the pig left the stable.

A seven-year-old Australian boy was at the centre of a New South Wales courtroom drama when he challenged a court ruling over who should have custody over him. The boy had a history of being beaten by his parents and the judge initially awarded custody to an aunt, in keeping with child custody regulations requiring that family unity should be maintained to the best degree possible.

The boy surprised the court when he proclaimed that the aunt beat him more than his parents and he adamantly refused to live with her. When the judge then suggested that he live with his grandparents, the boy cried out that they also beat him.

After considering the remainder of the immediate family and learning that domestic violence was apparently a way of life among them, the judge took the unprecedented step of allowing the boy to decide who should have custody of him.

After two recesses to check legal references and confer with child welfare officials, the judge granted temporary custody of the boy to the England cricket team whom the boy firmly believes are not capable of beating anyone.

The Liberal Democrats' lament.

Ten Liberal Democrats trying to align
One only did so – and then there were nine.

Nine Liberal Democrats entered a debate
One spoke his heart out – and then there were eight

Eight Liberal Democrats saw the road to Heaven
One tried to follow it – and then there were seven

Seven Liberal Democrats trying hard to mix
One got all mixed up – and then there were six

Six Liberal Democrats eager to survive
One turned a somersault – and then there were five

Five Liberal Democrats found they had the floor
One spoke for all of them – and then there were four

Four Liberal Democrats sitting down to tea

One choked on a principle – and then there were three

Three Liberal Democrats looking at the view
One found a policy – and then there were two

Two Liberal Democrats politically outrun
One lost his deposit – and then there was one

One Liberal Democrat found nothing could be done
So he caught a plane to China – and then there were none.

A photographer hated wearing his seat belt, but one day he spotted a police car and decided to put it on quickly. ' Here, take the wheel,' he told his wife. She did, but it was too late and he was pulled over. 'I noticed you weren't wearing your seat belt,' the officer said. 'Yes I was,' he answered. ' But don't take my word for it. Ask my wife.' 'Madam?' enquired the policeman. 'Officer, I've been married to him for 20 years,' she replied. 'And one thing I've learnt in all that time is never to argue with him when he is drunk.'

An American evangelist once had wires connected to all the seats in the UK church he was visiting. 'All those who are willing to give £200 to God, ' he shouted,' stand up!' As he said this he pressed a button and electricity zapped through the seats. There was a tremendous response, but later the church stewards found three dead Scotsmen clinging to their pews.

Every day at precisely 10.32am a newspaper editor would leave whatever he was doing in the news room and go back into his office from where he could see the Inter-City express rush past the window. No matter what he was doing at the time he would always watch the train as it flashed past. One day the chief reporter on behalf of the other journalists decided to ask him why he carried out such an unusual ritual. ' Isn't your hobby getting a little out of hand' he enquired. 'Oh, I'm not interested in train-spotting,' he explained. 'I just like to see the only thing that moves in this area without me having to push it.'

A Welshman was stranded on a desert island for 20 years. At last he was rescued by a merchant ship blown off-course during a storm. Arriving on the island, the sailors were amazed to see that the Welshman had not only built himself a finely constructed timber house, but a village with all sorts of amenities. There was a shop, a hall, a drinking fountain – and two chapels. 'What's the other chapel for?' they asked. The Welshman replied sternly: ' That's the one I don't go to.'

A beautiful blonde actress arrived in Heaven. St Cedric, who was on reception that decade, was extremely surprised to see her considering her infamous reputation on earth. 'Are you sure you've come to the right place?' he asked. The actress smiled seductively. 'I went to an evangelistic rally where I was converted just before I died,' she explained. 'These rallies are going too far these days,' murmured St Cedric.' Life was much tougher in my days. Very well but you'll have to walk ahead of me down that long corridor into Heaven and if you have one single naughty thought a trap door will open and you'll drop down to the other place.' So the actress walked off down the corridor swaying her hips. About halfway along a trap door opened and St Cedric fell through.

Three Englishmen were sitting together and bragging about how they had given their new wives duties to perform.

Terry had married an American woman and bragged that he had told his wife she needed to do all the dishes and housework. He said that it took a couple of days but on the third day he came home to a clean house and the dishes were all washed and put away.

Jimmy had married a Canadian woman and he bragged that he had given his wife orders that she had to do all the cleaning, dishes and the cooking. He told them that the first day he didn't see any results, but the next day it was better. By the third day his house was clean, the dishes were done and he had a huge dinner on the table.

The third man had married a woman from Yorkshire. He boasted that he told her that her duties were to keep the house cleaned, dishes washed, do the laundry and ironing twice a week, mow the lawn, clean the windows and have hot meals on the table for every meal.

He said the first day he didn't see anything, the second day he didn't see anything but by the third day most of the swelling had gone down and he could see a little out of his left eye, just enough to fix himself a bite to eat, load the dishwasher and call a handyman.

It's late fall and the Indians on a remote reservation in North Dakota asked their new chief if the coming winter was going to be cold or mild. Since he was a chief in a modern society, he had never been taught the old secrets. When he looked at the sky, he couldn't tell what the winter was going to be like.

Nevertheless, to be on the safe side, he told his tribe that the winter was indeed going to be cold and that the members of the village should collect firewood to be prepared. But also being a practical leader, after several days, he got an idea. He went to the phone booth, called the National Weather Service and asked, 'Is

the coming winter going to be cold?'

'It looks like this winter is going to be quite cold,' the meteorologist at the weather service responded. So the chief went back to his people and told them to collect even more firewood in order to be prepared.

A week later, he called the National Weather Service again. 'Does it still look like it is going to be a very cold winter?' 'Yes,' the man at National Weather Service again replied, 'it's going to be a very cold winter.' The chief again went back to his people and ordered them to collect every scrap of firewood they could find.

Two weeks later, the chief called the National Weather Service again. 'Are you absolutely sure that the winter is going to be very cold?' 'Absolutely,' the man replied. 'It's looking more and more like it is going to be one of the coldest winters we've ever seen.'

'How can you be so sure?' the chief asked. The weatherman replied, 'The Indians are collecting a massive amount of firewood'

After Quasimodo's death, the bishop of the Cathedral of Notre Dame sent word through the streets of Paris that a new bell ringer was needed. After observing several applicants demonstrate their skills, he had decided to call it a day. Just then, an armless man approached him and announced that he was there to apply for the bell ringer's job. The bishop was incredulous.

'You have no arms !' 'No matter,' said the man. 'Observe !' And he began striking the bells with his face, producing a beautiful melody on the carillon. The bishop listened in astonishment; convinced he had finally found a replacement for Quasimodo.

But suddenly, as he rushed forward to strike the bell, the armless man tripped and plunged headlong out of the belfry window to his death in the street below. The stunned bishop rushed down two hundred and ninety five church steps. When he reached the street, a crowd had gathered around the fallen figure, drawn by the beautiful music they had heard only moment before.

As they silently parted to let the bishop through, one of them asked, 'Bishop, who was this man ?' 'I don't know his name,' the bishop sadly replied, 'But his face rings a bell.'

The following day, despite the sadness that weighed heavily on his heart due to the unfortunate death of the armless campanologist, the bishop continued his interviews for the bell ringer of Notre Dame. The first man to approach him said, 'Your Excellency, I am the brother of the poor armless wretch that fell to his death from this very belfry yesterday. I pray that you honour his life by allowing me to replace him in this duty.'

The bishop agreed to give the man an audition, and, as the armless man's brother stooped to pick up a mallet to strike the first bell, he groaned, clutched at his chest, twirled around, and died on the spot. Two monks, hearing the bishop's cries of grief at this second tragedy, rushed up the stairs to his side. 'What has happened ? Who is this man ?' the first monk asked breathlessly. 'I don't know his name,' sighed the distraught bishop, 'but....' He's a dead ringer for his brother.'

Two beggars are sitting side by side on a street in Rome . One has a Cross in front of him; the other is holding the Star of David. Many people go by, look at both beggars, but only put money into the hat of the beggar sitting behind the Cross. The Pope comes by. He stops to watch the throngs of people giving money to the beggar who holds the Cross while none give to the beggar holding the Star of David. Finally, the Pope approaches the beggar with the Star of David and says: "My poor fellow, don't you understand? This is a Catholic country; this city is the Seat of Catholicism. People aren't going to give you money if you sit there with a Star

of David in front of you, especially when you're sitting beside a beggar who is holding a Cross. In fact, they would probably give more money to him just out of spite." The beggar with the Star of David listened to the Pope, smiled, and turned to the beggar with the Cross and said, "Moishe, look who's trying to teach the Goldstein brothers about marketing!"

A big Norwegian mountain guy stopped at a local restaurant following a day roaming around in Spain on holiday.   While sipping his wine, he noticed a sizzling, scrumptious looking platter being served at the next table Not only did it look good, but the smell was wonderful. He asked the waiter, 'What is that you just served?'

The waiter replied, 'Si Senor, you have excellent taste! Those are called Cojones de Toro, bull's testicles from the bull fight this morning. A delicacy!' The Norwegian said, 'What the heck, bring me an order.'

The waiter replied, 'I am so sorry senor. There is only one serving per day because there is only one bull fight each morning. If you come early and place your order, we will be sure to save you this delicacy.'

The next morning, the Norwegian returned, placed his order, and that evening was served the
one and only special delicacy of the day.   After a few bites, inspecting his platter, he called to the waiter and said, 'These are delicious, but they are much, much smaller than the ones I saw you serve yesterday.'

The waiter shrugged his shoulders and replied, 'Si, Senor. Sometimes the bull wins."

After being married for thirty years, a wife asked her husband to describe her.

He looked at her for awhile ... then said, "You're A, B, C, D, E, F, G, H, I, J, K."

She asks ... "What does that mean?"

He said, "Adorable, Beautiful, Cute, Delightful, Elegant, Foxy, Gorgeous, and Hot".

She smiled happily and said ... "Oh, that's so lovely ... What about I, J, K?"

He said, "I'm Just kidding!"

The swelling in his eye is going down, and the doctor is fairly optimistic about his nose.

There was a knock on the door this morning. I opened it to find a young man standing there who said: "Hello Sir, I'm a Jehovah's Witness ." I said "Come in and sit down." I offered him coffee and asked, "What do you want to talk about?" He said, "Blowed if I know, I've never got this far before!"

It was the Scotland/Wales rugby International weekend in Edinburgh and as the crowds made their way down Princes Street towards Murrayfield, a Rottweiler suddenly lunged towards an eight year old Scottish lass, with its jaws wide open ready to attack.

The crowd nearby gasped in horror but, quick as a flash, a man in red jumped out of the crowd, grabbed the dog by the throat and throttled it. As the dead dog lay there and the crowd cheered in admiration, a journalist from The Scotsman, who had witnessed the heroic deed, went up to the man and said 'That was brilliant, I can see the headline now - 'Welsh Rugby Fan Saves Young Girl From Certain Death'.

The man replied, 'No, you've got it wrong. I'm not here for the rugby!'

'Don't worry' said the journalist, 'I can see the headline now - 'Welshman Saves Girl From Jaws Of Rottweiler'.

The man replied, 'No, you're wrong again. I'm not Welsh; I'm from London

The journalist said, 'Don't worry; I can see the headline now - 'English thug strangles family pet'.

I dialled a number and got the following recording: "I am not available right now, but thank you for caring enough to call. I am making some changes in life. Please leave a message after the Beep. If I do not return your call, you one of the changes."

A driver was stuck in a traffic jam on the M25 near London . Nothing was moving. Suddenly, a man knocks on the window. The driver rolls down the window and asks, "What's going on?"

"Terrorists have kidnapped all members of Parliament, and they're asking a £100 million ransom. Otherwise, they are going to douse them all in petrol and set them on fire. We are going from car to car, collecting donations."

"How much is everyone giving, on an average?" the driver asks. The man replies, "Roughly a litre."

A number of jokes suitable for a speaking engagement involving more senior folk.

An elderly gentleman had serious hearing problems for a number of years. He went to the doctor
and the doctor was able to have him fitted for a set of hearing aids that allowed the gentleman to hear 100% The elderly gentleman went back in a month to the doctor and the doctor said, 'Your hearing is perfect.. Your family must be really pleased that you can hear again.' The gentleman replied, 'Oh, I haven't told my family yet. I just sit around and listen to the conversations. I've changed my will three times!'

Two elderly gentlemen from a retirement centre were sitting on a bench under a tree when one turns to the other and says: 'Bill, I'm 83 years old now and I'm just full of aches and pains. I know you're about my age. How do you feel?' Bill says, 'I feel just like a newborn baby.' 'Really!? Like a newborn baby!?' 'Yep. No hair, no teeth, and I think I just wet my pants.'

An elderly couple had dinner at another couple's house, and after eating, the wives left the table and went into the kitchen. The two gentlemen were talking, and one said, 'Last night we went out to a new restaurant and it was really great... I would recommend it very highly.'

The other man said, 'What is the name of the restaurant?'

The first man thought and thought and finally said, 'What is the name of that flower you give to someone you love? You know... The one that's red and has thorns.'

'Do you mean a rose?' 'Yes, that's the one,' replied the man. He then turned

towards the kitchen and yelled, 'Rose, what's the name of that restaurant w
went to last night?'

**Some hospital regulations require a wheel chair for patients being
discharged. However, a student nurse found one elderly gentleman alread
dressed and sitting on the bed with a suitcase at his feet, who insisted he
didn't need any help to leave the hospital. After a chat about rules being
rules, he reluctantly let the student nurse wheel him to the elevator. On th
way down she asked him if his wife was meeting him. 'I don't know,' he sai
'She's still upstairs in the bathroom changing out of her hospital gown.'**

A couple in their nineties are both having problems remembering things.
During a checkup, the doctor tells them that they're physically okay, but the
might want to start writing things down to help them remember.

Later that night, while watching TV, the old man gets up from his chair. 'Wan
anything while I'm in the kitchen?' he asks. 'Will you get me a bowl of ice
cream?' 'Sure..'

'Don't you think you should write it down so you can remember it?' she asks

'No, I can remember it.'

'Well, I'd like some strawberries on top, too. Maybe you should write it dow
so as not to forget it?'

He says, 'I can remember that. You want a bowl of ice cream with
strawberries.'

I'd also like whipped cream. I'm certain you'll forget that, write it down?' she asks.

Irritated, he says, 'I don't need to write it down, I can remember it! Ice cream with strawberries and whipped cream - I got it, for goodness sake!'

Then he toddles into the kitchen. After about 20 minutes, the old man returns from the kitchen and hands his wife a plate of bacon and eggs. She stares at the plate for a moment. And says, 'Where's my toast ?'

A senior citizen said to his eighty-year old buddy: 'So I hear you're getting married?' 'Yep!'

'Do I know her?' 'Nope!'

'This woman, is she good looking?' 'Not really.'

'Is she a good cook?' 'Naw, she can't cook too well.'

'Does she have lots of money?' 'Nope! Poor as a church mouse.'

'Well, then, is she good in bed?' 'I don't know.'

'Why in the world do you want to marry her then?' 'Because she can still drive!'

Bob receives a free ticket to the FA Cup Final from his company. Unfortunately, when he arrives at the stadium he realises the seat is in the last row in the corner of the stadium. About halfway through the first half, Bob notices an empty seat five rows off the pitch right on the halfway line. He decides to ta a chance and makes his way through the stadium and around the security guards to the empty seat.

As he sits down, he asks the elderly gentleman sitting next to him, "Excuse r is anyone sitting here?" The man says no. Now, very excited to be in suc great seat for the game, Bob again inquires of the man next to him, "Thi incredible! Who in their right mind would have a seat like this for the Cup Fi and not use it?" The man replies, "Well, actually, the seat belongs to me, I w supposed to come with my wife, but she passed away. This is the first C Final we haven't been to together since we got married in 1962."

"Well, that's really sad," says Bob, "but still, couldn't you find someone to ta the seat? A relative or a close friend?" "No," the man replies, "they're all at funeral.

An old man lay sprawled across three entire seats in the movie theatre. When the usher came by and noticed this, he whispered to the old man... "Sorry sir, but you're only allowed ONE seat!" The old man didn't budge.

The usher became more impatient... "Sir, if you don't get up from there I'm going to have to call the manager."

Once again, the old man just muttered and did nothing!

The usher marched briskly back up the aisle, and in a moment he returned with the manager.

Together the two of them tried repeatedly to move the old dishevelled ma but with no success!

Finally they summoned the police. The officer surveyed the situation briefly then asked....... "All right

buddy what's your name?" "Fred," the old man moaned.

"Where ya' from, Fred?" asked the police officer.

With a terrible grunt in his voice, and without moving, Fred replied...... "The balcony!"

Morris, an 82 year-old man, went to the doctor to get a physical. A few days later, the doctor saw Morris walking down the street with a gorgeous young woman on his arm. A couple of days later, the doctor spoke to Morris and said, 'You're really doing great, aren't you?'

Morris replied, 'Just doing what you said, Doc: 'Get a hot mamma and be cheerful.''

The doctor said, 'I didn't say that.. I said, 'You've got a heart murmur; be careful.'

A little old man shuffled slowly into an ice cream parlour and pulled himself slowly, painfully, up onto a stool... After catching his breath, he ordered a banana split. The waitress asked kindly, 'Crushed nuts?' 'No,' he replied, 'Arthritis.'

CHAPTER EIGHT

SHORT JOKES

and ONE LINERS

"I don't mind making jokes, but I don't want to look like one." —
Marilyn Monroe

Two guys were discussing popular family trends on sex, marriage, and family values. Bill said, 'I didn't sleep with my wife before we got married, did you?' Larry replied, 'I'm not sure, what was her maiden name?'

A little boy went up to his father and asked: 'Dad, where did my intelligence come from?'The father replied. 'Well, son, you must have got it from your mother, cause I still have mine.'

'Mr. Clark, I have reviewed this case very carefully,' the divorce court judge said, 'And I've decided to give your wife £575 a week,' 'That's very fair, my lud,' the husband said. 'And every now and then I'll try to send her a few pounds myself.'

A doctor examining a woman who had been rushed to the emergency room, took the husband aside, and said, 'I don't like the looks of your wife at all. ''Me neither doc,' said the husband. 'But she's a great cook and really good with the kids.'

An old man goes to the Wizard to ask him if he can remove a curse he has been living with for the last 40 years. The Wizard says, 'Maybe, but you will have to tell me the exact words that were used to put the curse on you.' The old man says without hesitation, 'I now pronounce you man and wife.'

A blonde calls Virgin Atlantic and asks, 'Can you tell me how long it'll take to fly from London to New York City ?' The agent replies, 'Just a minute.' 'Thank you,' the blonde says, and hangs up.

Two detectives were investigating the murder of Juan Gonzalez. 'How was he killed?' asked one detective. 'With a golf gun,' the other detective replied. 'A golf gun! What is a golf gun?' 'I don't know. But it sure made a hole in Juan.'

Moe: 'My wife got me to believe in religion.' Joe: 'Really?' Moe: 'Yeah. Until I married her I didn't believe in Hell.'

A man is recovering from surgery when the Surgical Nurse appears and asks him how he is feeling. 'I'm O. K. But I didn't like the four letter-words the doctor used insurgery,' he answered. 'What did he say,' asked the nurse. 'Oops!'

While shopping for holiday clothes, my husband and I passed a display of bathing suits. It had been at least ten years and twenty pounds since I had even considered buying a bathing suit, so I sought my husband's advice. 'What do you think?' I asked. 'Should I get a bikini or an all-in-one?'

'Better get a bikini,' he replied. 'You'd never get it all in one. He's still in intensive care.

The graveside service just barely finished, when there was massive clap of thunder, followed by a tremendous bolt of lightning, accompanied by Even more thunder rumbling in the distance... The grieving husband looked at the pastor and calmly said, 'Well, she's there!'

Humpty Dumpty sat on a wall

Humpty Dumpty had a great fall

The structure of the wall was incorrect

So he got a grand from Claims Direct

Mary had a little lamb

Her father shot it dead

Now it goes to school with her

Between two chunks of bread

My wife told me I was no longer romantic so I booked a table for us on Valentine's night. Problem was she is rubbish at snooker.

I have kleptomania, but when it gets bad I take something for it.

There are two periods in a man's life when he does not understand a woman – before he's married and after he's married.

Heaven is where the police are British, the chefs Italian, the mechanics are German, the lovers are French and it's all organised by the Swiss. Hell is where the police are German, the chefs are

British, the mechanics are French, the lovers are Swiss and it's all organised by the Italians.

Favourite headline: *Suicidal twin kills sister by mistake.*

In just two days from now, tomorrow will be yesterday.

German Chancellor Angela Merkel went on holiday to Greece. At immigration she was asked: ' Occupation?' To which she replied ' Not this time! '

It was meal time during an airline flight. 'Would you like dinner?' the flight attendant asked John seated in front. 'What are my choices,' asked John. 'Yes or no,' she replied.

A friend of mine thinks everyone should get married because no-one deserves to be happy their entire life.

My wife had her credit card stolen last week but I have decided not to report it to the police because the thief is spending less than she was.

Three old guys are out walking. First one says, 'Windy, isn't it?' Second one says, 'No, it's Thursday!' Third one says, 'So am I. Let's go get a beer.'

A man was telling his neighbour, 'I just bought a new hearing aid. It cost me four thousand pounds, but it's state of the art.. It's perfect.' 'Really,' answered the neighbour . 'What kind is it?'

'Twelve thirty..'

Frustration is trying to find your glasses without your glasses.

The irony of life is that, by the time you're old enough to know your way around, you're not going anywhere.

I was always taught to respect my elders, but it keeps getting harder to find one.

At the Irish wedding reception the D.J. yelled..."Would all married men please stand next to the one person who has made your life worth living." The bartender was almost crushed to death.

With all the sadness and trauma going on in the world at the moment, it is worth reflecting on the death of Larry LaPrise, the man who wrote ' The Hokey Cokey' who died peacefully at the age of 93. The most traumatic part for his family was getting him in the coffin. They put his left leg in ... and then the trouble started.

Just got off the phone with a friend who lives in Minot , Minnesota . He said that since early this morning the snow has been nearly waist high and is still falling. The temperature is 32 below zero and the north wind is increasing to near gale force. Wind chill is -59. His wife has done nothing but look through the kitchen window and just stare. He says that if it gets much worse, he may have to let her in.

THE END

www.ingramcontent.com/pod-product-compliance
Lightning Source LLC
Chambersburg PA
CBHW062208280526
45788CB00001B/499